Film Funding SECRETS

For Independent

Filmmakers

By

Douglas Vermeeren

Bulk copies of this book may be ordered for educational purposes through Ridley Jones Publisher.

This book and the information contained therein is part of the Film Funding Blueprint programs for funding independent film.

Disclaimer: The author makes no claim to be a financial advisor by sharing this information. This information is based exclusively on his own personal experiences and makes no guarantee of funding success through the use of this information. The author encourages all filmmakers to do their own due diligence with any of the information shared herein. Each film project is different and unique and may have significant differences or requirements based on legal restrictions in your geographical area, the amount of funding you are looking to raise, and with those who are willing to provide your funding. Please consult with your own legal resources and accounting team to determine your specific requirements. No part of this book may be copied without the express written consent of the author and publisher.

TABLE OF CONTENTS

Chapter 1

THE REAL BEGINNING: WHY THIS BOOK EXISTS AND WHY YOU'RE HERE

Every filmmaker eventually reaches the same crossroads, the moment where the script is ready, the passion is alive, the team is forming, and momentum feels unstoppable...except for one thing: the money isn't there.

This moment is universal. It doesn't matter whether you're making a $2,500 short film or a $3 million feature. It doesn't matter if you're brand new or you've been in the industry for decades. Every project eventually arrives at this place where inspiration collides with the financial reality of filmmaking.

That's why I'm writing this book.

Over the years, I've met thousands of filmmakers: students, first time directors, seasoned producers, YouTubers, cinematographers ready to make their first feature, documentarians, and visionary storytellers. Almost every one of them told me the same thing:

"I know the film I want to make. I just don't know how to fund it."

They don't lack creativity. They don't lack drive.

What they lack is **a map.**

The filmmaking world is full of myths, misunderstandings, bad advice, and outdated strategies around funding. Too many filmmakers are being taught ideas that simply don't work. They're told funding is impossible. They're told no one funds shorts. They're told that the only way to raise money is to beg, or sacrifice ownership, or chase investors who don't care.

I've seen the frustration.

I've lived it.

And I've helped hundreds of others climb out of that confusion.

This book exists because filmmakers desperately need clarity, direction, and actual *support* in the most important—and ironically one of the easiest—to-fix aspects of filmmaking: **raising the money.**

Why I Am Writing This Book

There are three reasons:

1. Filmmakers deserve real answers—not myths.

The industry has no shortage of loud opinions. The problem is that most of them are wrong. Many of the "rules" filmmakers are told are simply inherited beliefs from others who struggled—or never tried effectively.

People say:

- *"You can't raise money for a short film."*

- *"You need private investors."*

- *"Only established filmmakers get funding."*

- *"Nobody funds documentaries."*

- *"You must have a star first."*

Every one of these statements is incorrect.

There are funding partners for every kind of project.

Shorts. Documentaries. Low-budget features.

High-concept features. Verticals. Series pilots. Even experimental or artistic films.

Filmmakers simply need someone to show them where these partners exist, how they think, and how to communicate with them.

That's why this book exists.

2. Poor guidance can kill a filmmaker's dream—even when the dream is fully achievable.

I've watched passion die in filmmakers because they were given bad advice. I've seen people walk away from brilliant ideas because they thought funding would take years... or that only "Hollywood people" get deals... or that their idea wasn't good enough.

Yet I've repeatedly watched filmmakers fund projects once they understood how money actually works in this business.

All they needed was the correct information.

All they needed was someone to explain it simply.

All they needed was a system they could follow.

I've spent decades teaching this material at workshops, film schools, festivals, and private programs. Over the years, I've heard the same feedback:

"This changed everything for me."

"No one talks about funding this way."

"I got my project funded because of this."

Filmmakers are hungry for clear guidance. This book is an answer to that need.

3. I've done this for decades, and the results speak for themselves.

I've been fortunate to raise funding for many types of films, in many genres, in many formats. My first film, "The Opus," was raised entirely from private funding partners, over $600,000. That film went on to be translated into more than 26 languages, distributed worldwide, and published as a book in an equal number of languages.

That film launched my career.

But more importantly, it showed me what's actually possible.

Since then, I've repeated the process again and again:

- Additional personal development documentaries.

- Narrative features in a variety of genres.

- Short films for new and emerging creators.

- Vertical films and new-media formats.

- TV pilots.

- Micro-budget projects as small as $2,500.

- Larger independent productions up to $3 million.

- Collaborations with filmmakers across Canada, the USA, Europe, and beyond.

Along the way, I discovered the patterns.

The principles.

The strategies that allowed films of any size to get funded by the right partners.

I've used them.

I've taught them.

I've watched others succeed with them.

Now I want to put them in your hands.

Why I Am Qualified To Write This Book

I'm not writing this book based on theory, textbooks, or wishful thinking.

Everything you're about to learn comes from real experience, over two decades of it.

Here's what qualifies me:

1. **I have personally raised millions of dollars for films.**

I know where money comes from, how to access it, and how to talk to people who have it. I know how they think, what they expect, and what makes them say yes.

2. **My films have succeeded—creatively, financially, and internationally.**

"The Opus" and the films that followed weren't just funded, they reached global audiences.

That matters.

Because repeatability is everything in filmmaking.

3. **I've helped filmmakers at every level.**

From a $2,500 short to a multimillion-dollar feature, I've helped filmmakers secure the funds they needed. Not once. Not twice. But consistently, for years.

4. **I've taught this material to thousands of people.**

Film schools.

Workshops. Industry events. Private mentorship programs.

People don't just like learning this, they rely on it.

5. **My strategies are simple, practical, and proven.**

Filmmakers walk away with real funding partners, real money, and real results. Not theory. Not "Hollywood magic."

As a side note, I might mention that I am on the advisory board of the American Film Convention and supervise their speed pitching activities. Each year, I see more than 600 filmmakers share their best pitches and pleas to get money from potential film funders. Most often, they are not successful. Witnessing these mistakes has given me some keen insights into why potential film funders give money to some projects and avoid others. I will share those insights here.

On a second note, I have been teaching filmmakers the things I have learned about film funding for several decades now. Some have been very successful. I have been part of funding everything from shorts, documentaries, narrative features, and television pilots. As I have taught others, I have also been a student. I have learned from the creativity of filmmakers who have taken some of my ideas and added new and interesting twists. This has been interesting to see.

And of course, along the way, I have also learned about new kinds of film funding partners and why they fund movies.

These systems and effective tactics are what you will get here.

That's why I'm writing this book. Because this information works. Because it is needed.

Because it has already changed lives and careers.

And because it will change yours, too, if you apply it.

YES, YOU CAN RAISE MONEY FOR SHORTS

Let's address one of the biggest myths immediately:

You absolutely, unquestionably, 100% can raise money for short films.

People do it all the time.

Shorts are:

- Easier to complete.

- Less risky than features.

- Perfect testing grounds for new ideas.

- Marketable within festivals and online distribution.

- Valuable calling cards for careers.

There are countless funding partners who love supporting shorts:

- Local businesses

- Community organizations

- Nonprofits

- Special-interest groups

- *Schools and universities*

- *Professional associations*

- *Brands*

- *Networks*

- *Foundations*

Filmmakers say "you can't raise money for shorts" only because they've never been taught how to do it.

You can. This book will show you how.

What You Can Expect From This Book

If you apply what you learn, here is what will happen:

1. You will understand how people with money actually make decisions.

Not based on emotion, luck, or pressure. Based on logic, incentive, safety, relationship, and opportunity.

2. You will learn how to become someone funding partners want to support.

Not because your film is pretty, but because you understand how to speak their language.

3. You will gain the confidence to ask for funding without fear.

Because confidence comes from clarity, and clarity comes from knowing what works.

4. You will build real relationships with potential funding partners.

Relationships that extend far beyond one film.

5. You will stop seeing funding as a mysterious barrier—and start seeing it as a skill.

A skill you can master.

This is a skill that will serve your entire career. Funding will often determine which films get made and how quickly they can be made. Ask any filmmaker, and you'll generally find that funding is the bottleneck that consumes most of the process of making a film. Most often, funding the film is even a much lengthier process than writing the script. It makes sense to get good at this essential part of filmmaking so that you can establish a team that will fund your films frequently and fast.

What This Book Is Not

This book is *not* a get-rich-quick scheme. It is not a magic wand.

It will not fund your film for you. This book is a guideline to help you consider and organize your film project in a way that makes it fundable.

Funding takes:

- Preparation

- Time

- Communication Skill

- Strategy

- Relationship-Building

- *Persistence*

- *Follow-Through*

People who have money expect you to be prepared.

They expect clarity.

They expect professionalism.

They expect you to treat your filmmaking like a business, not a hobby.

If you want shortcuts, this isn't the book.

If you want results, this absolutely is.

Creativity Precedes Funding

One of the most important principles in this book is this:

Funding follows creativity.

People don't fund film scripts, they fund creative visions explained well.

The best ideas get funded.

But only when they are communicated clearly and effectively.

The question is not simply:

"Do you have a good idea?"

The real question is:

"Can you share it in a way that others immediately understand, believe in, and want to participate in?"

Creativity matters.

But communication is what converts creativity into funding.

Relationships Precede Funding

Another foundational truth that is essential to funding your film:

Money people fund creative people, not just creative ideas.

The idea matters, but the person matters more.

Your funding partner is not investing in:

- Your Script

- Your Camera Package

- Your Mood Board

- Your Deck

- Your Cast List

- Your Festival Plan

They are investing in you—the filmmaker who will steer this ship.

That means:

- Integrity Matters

- Consistency Matters

- *Communication Matters*

- *Professionalism Matters*

- *Follow-Through Matters*

Relationships create funding.

Funding does not create relationships.

Funding Happens Twice

Most filmmakers only think about funding once, when they're trying to get the money to make the film.

But a film is actually funded twice:

1. Funding to make and market the film

This includes the budget, production costs, post-production, deliverables, legal, marketing, advertising, festival submissions, and everything required to get the film completed and seen.

2. Funding when audiences "buy in"

This happens through:

- *Ticket Sales*

- *Festival Attendance*

- *Distribution*

- *Licensing*

- *Streaming Sales*

- *Merchandis*

- *Partnerships,*

- *Sponsorships*

- *Community Engagement*

From day one, you must think about both. I will talk primarily about the first one in this book. But you should definitely be thinking about your audience from the beginning. Thinking about your audience will also help the potential film funding partners in the first group feel more confident that you are a safe bet for their investment.

Remember, the ultimate goal isn't just to get money from a potential film funding partner. The goal is to make a movie that benefits everyone. The better you prepare early, the more money will be drawn to your film later.

This is why we treat film funding like a business activity, not just a creative one.

Why Funding Is The Number One Thing Holding Filmmakers Back

The ironic truth is this:

Funding feels like the hardest part of filmmaking, but only because most filmmakers don't understand how it works.

When you learn what people with money want, how they evaluate opportunities, and what makes them *participate... suddenly, funding becomes one of the easiest problems to solve.*

Not effortless.

But absolutely doable.

Predictable.

Masterable.

I've watched filmmakers go from stuck to fully funded in weeks, not because of luck, but because they applied the right strategy.

You can too.

Why We Say "Funding Partner," Not "Investor"

Language matters.

The word "investor" scares filmmakers and funding partners alike. It carries heavy expectations, legal implications, and a mindset of high-risk capital.

The term "funding partner" is more accurate for most indie film deals.

A funding partner can be:

- A brand

- A business

- A nonprofit

- A community group

- A private sponsor

- A government program

- A foundation

- A professional association

- Or yes... sometimes a traditional investor.

Different partners bring different incentives and decision-making criteria.

Understanding these differences is the key to unlocking funding in ways most filmmakers never consider.

You'll also notice throughout this book and in my trainings and seminars, I often refer to the film funding partner as a POTENTIAL film funding partner. This is simply because they are potential partners until they actually give you money. I think it's important to think of them as potential partners because it helps you to remember that you and your project are being evaluated at all times. People shift to funding partners when you have given them enough reasons to trust you with their money and resources.

Raising Money Requires Thinking Like A Business Owner

This is another critical concept.

Filmmakers often approach fundraising like artists, hoping people will love their idea enough to throw money at it.

But filmmaking is not only an art. It is also a business.

In fact, when raising money, it is primarily a business.

Funding partners say yes when they see:

- Opportunity

- Return

- Alignment

- Benefit

- Reduced Risk

- A confident filmmaker who knows what they're doing

You are not selling a script. You are selling a business opportunity wrapped inside a creative vision.

When you learn to speak the language of business, suddenly funding becomes much easier.

The More Success You Build, The Easier Funding Becomes

Reputation is one of the strongest tools in your toolbox.

Every successful film you complete, whether it's a 3-minute short or a full feature, strengthens your ability to raise money again.

Funding partners trust track records. They trust reliability. They trust consistency. When you build a history of completing what you start, your funding conversations become dramatically easier.

But here's the good news: you don't need a long career to begin.

You only need one good project.

One well-communicated idea.

One clear pitch.

One well-executed short.

One meaningful relationship.

That's all it takes to start.

The Methods In This Book Fund Everything

The strategies you're about to learn have helped filmmakers fund:

- *Short films*

- *Documentaries*

- *Features*

- *New media projects*

- *Vertical films*

- *Series pilots*

- *Experimental projects*

- *Branded content*

- *Micro-budget films*

- *Multimillion-dollar independent features*

The principles are universal.

They don't depend on genre, location, or experience level.

They depend on clarity, creativity, communication, and relationships.

This book will teach you all of that.

25 Important Questions A Filmmaker Should Ask:

1. *Why is film funding often misunderstood in the industry?*

2. *What incorrect ideas have I personally believed about funding?*

3. *Have I been approaching funding as an artist or as a business owner?*

4. *What creative elements of my project make it fundable?*

5. *How well can I explain the value of my film to a funding partner?*

6. *Who would benefit from supporting my film?*

7. *What is my current reputation as a filmmaker, and does it help or hurt my funding efforts?*

8. *What short film or previous project could I leverage to build credibility?*

9. *Have I identified potential funding partners beyond traditional investors?*

10. *Do I understand how people with money think about opportunity and risk?*

11. *Do I know what incentives matter most to different types of partners?*

12. *Am I prepared to communicate professionally with funding partners?*

13. *Have I defined the business opportunity inside my film?*

14. *What makes me personally fundable—not just the script?*

15. *How much preparation have I done before asking for money?*

16. *Am I thinking about both stages of funding: creation and distribution?*

17. *What relationships do I already have that could lead to funding?*

18. *What relationships do I need to start building right now?*

19. *How will I demonstrate reliability and follow-through to funding partners?*

20. *What myths about fundraising have held me back?*

21. *What success stories from my own life can strengthen my pitch?*

22. *What emotional reason makes me want to make this project, and can I express it?*

23. *What logical reason would convince a funding partner to support it?*

24. *How can I make my project attractive to multiple different types of funding partners?*

25. *What first step can I take today to move closer to funding?*

HOW TO USE THE IDEAS IN THIS CHAPTER TO FUND YOUR FILM

Below are practical ways filmmakers can immediately apply the principles from this chapter.

1. Start thinking like a business owner.

Write a simple one-page outline describing the business opportunity behind your film:

- *Who it helps*

- *Why it matters*

- *What makes it unique*

- *How it will reach its audience*

- *Why a partner should care*

This alone will distinguish you from 90% of filmmakers.

2. Identify your potential funding partners.

Make a list of 30-50 groups that benefit from your film's theme or audience:

- *Local businesses*

- *Organizations*

- *Nonprofits*

- *Professional Groups*

- *Brands*

- *Community Centers*

- *Educational Institutions*

- *Associations*

- *Individuals with aligned values*

- *Influencers or thought leaders*

These are the real opportunities most filmmakers never see.

3. Build relationships before you need the money.

Reach out.

Connect.

Share updates.

Start conversations.

*Funding partners fund **people** they trust.*

4. Make your idea communicable.

Create:

- *A clean one-page overview*

- *A 60-second verbal pitch*

- *A simple visual deck*

If someone can understand your idea quickly, they can support it quickly.

5. Practice explaining your film without "filmmaker language"

Funding partners don't care about lenses, shots, or story beats.

Speak in terms of:

- *Impact*

- *Audience*

- *Distribution*

- *Purpose*

- *Partnership*

- *Opportunity*

When you adapt your communication to their world, they will listen.

6. Start small if needed

If you're new, fund a short first.

If you've made shorts, fund a feature next.

Each success builds your track record, and each track record multiplies your funding power.

7. Prepare for both stages of funding

Think ahead about:

- *Marketing*

- *Ticket Sales*

- *Audience Pathways*

- *Partnerships*

- *Distribution Channels*

- *Promotional Partners*

Funding partners want to see the full picture

8. Reframe your mindset

Stop believing funding is impossible. Start believing funding is a skill.

Skills can be learned. You're learning one right now.

Chapter 2

THE IMPORTANCE OF FUNDING

If the previous chapter established the "why" behind your desire to learn film funding, this chapter establishes the "why" behind the act of funding itself. And yes, this may seem obvious on the surface. Of course, every filmmaker knows movies need money. But most filmmakers misunderstand how money works in this industry, why people fund films, and what separates the projects that get supported from the ones that never leave the laptop.

The truth is simple:

Movies don't get made without funding. Movies get made because someone believed.

Funding is not just a financial exchange, it is an act of support, belief, alignment, and collaboration· It is one of the most powerful forms of validation a filmmaker can receive·

And it is the lifeblood of every project, from the smallest micro-budget short to the biggest blockbuster·

In this chapter, we're going to peel back the curtain on what funding really is, why it matters, and why the presence or absence of funding is often the deciding factor between a dream fulfilled and a dream abandoned·

Movies Don't Get Made Without Funding And Support

Every filmmaker shares the same fantasy: rushing into production fueled by passion, creativity, and artistic fire· But filmmaking is not paint, or poetry, or a lonely afternoon with a notebook· Filmmaking is collaborative·

It requires people, equipment, food, locations, technology, safety, travel, time, and the ability to compensate others for their skill and effort. Everything in filmmaking costs money. Everything requires support. When you look at the thousands of films produced each year—yes, thousands, it becomes clear that funding is not rare.

Funding is everywhere. Across the world, people are funding films every single day. Films with big budgets, small budgets, odd budgets, experimental visions, unique audiences, and personal stories. The amount of movies being made today is proof that the marketplace is full of support. If people across the world are securing funding, then the question is no longer:

"Is funding available?"

The real question is:

"How do I access the support that already exists?"

If your project is solid, meaningful, creative, well-structured, and clearly communicated...someone will want to support you.

It's not a matter of luck. It's a matter of alignment.

But that requires you to understand what support actually means.

MOVIES ARE THE MOST EXPENSIVE ART FORM, AND ALSO ONE OF THE MOST LUCRATIVE

There is no cheaper artistic medium than a pencil and paper.

There is no more expensive artistic medium than filmmaking.

Even a simple three-minute short film can balloon in cost if a filmmaker isn't intentional.

And a feature film? It is, without exaggeration, the most expensive artistic pursuit available to the everyday creative.

But here is the other side of that coin:

Movies can also be one of the most lucrative opportunities available.

A great film can do many things. Aside from the entertainment value and influence of popular culture, here are a few important things to consider:

- Generate revenue for decades

- Create global cultural impact

- Attract sponsorships

- Be licensed repeatedly

- Sell merchandise

- Receive grants

- *Build a filmmaker's brand*

- *Serve as a business card for larger future opportunities*

And perhaps most importantly:

A film creates shared value for everyone involved.

The actors gain exposure.

The crew gains credits.

The locations benefit from business.

Communities gain pride.

Audiences gain value.

Sponsors gain visibility.

Funding partners gain reputational or financial returns.

Film has leverage.

Film has scale.

Film has reached.

This is why people are willing to fund films, because the upside is enormous when you know how to communicate it properly.

Why Funding Is Given To Specific Projects

One of the greatest misunderstandings filmmakers have is assuming people only fund films for financial return.

If money was the only deciding factor, most films would never get funded, because the financial outcome of a film is never guaranteed. The unpredictability of the entertainment industry means that returns can vary widely.

Yet every day, people fund films.

Why?

Because people fund people.

Because people fund vision.

Because people fund creation.

Money and returns matter.

Of course they do.

But for most funding partners, especially in the early stages—returns are not the primary motivator.

Here are the real motivators:

- Shared values

- Belief in your story

- Passion for the genre or message

- Excitement about the creative vision

- Desire to be part of something meaningful

- The prestige of association

- Community impact

- Their personal goals or identity

- The experience of participating

- Supporting local filmmakers

- *The desire to bring a message into the world*

The truth is:

People don't fund films. They fund the purpose.

They fund relationships.

They fund storytellers.

A business opportunity may open the door.

But the relationship and vision are what make someone step through it.

Different Levels of Funding Determine the Effectiveness of Your Production

Budget size is not just a number.

It is a creative decision.

More money doesn't automatically make a better film, but less money limits creative execution.

Filmmakers must understand the connection between funding, production quality, and audience experience.

A small budget can still produce a meaningful, powerful film, but it requires cleverness, discipline, and strategic choices.

Here's the truth most filmmakers don't want to admit:

Many good films fail because they were underfunded.

Many great films never get made for the same reason.

Funding gives you the ability to:

- Hire the right team

- Secure the right equipment

- Take the necessary time

- Choose better locations

- Enhance production design

- Elevate sound and audio quality

- *Invest in strong marketing*

- *Distribute effectively*

A small budget forces compromises.

A strong budget creates possibilities.

Funding is not everything, but it changes everything.

FUNDING IS OFTEN THE DIFFERENCE BETWEEN A MOVIE GETTING MADE AND NOT

I have watched brilliant scripts sit on hard drives for years because the filmmaker didn't know how to get funding.

I've also watched average scripts get fully funded simply because the filmmaker:

- *Prepared*

- *Communicated clearly*

- *Treated filmmaking like a business*

- *Built meaningful relationships*

- *Understood funding psychology*

- *Presented confidently*

Many filmmakers believe "if the idea is good, it will get made."

But the real statement is:

If the filmmaker is prepared, the idea will get funded.

Funding is the catalyst that transforms an idea into a reality.

Ideas are free.

Movies are not.

Funding Comes To Those Who Are Prepared

There is a predictable pattern across every filmmaker I've ever seen get funded. They were:

- *Prepared*

- *Organized*

- *Proactive*

- *Strategic*

- *Business-Minded*

Preparedness signals maturity.

Preparedness lowers risk.

Preparedness builds trust.

A filmmaker who shows up with:

- *A clear vision*

- *A strong pitch*

- *A professional deck*

- *A believable budget*

- *A strategic plan*

- *A distribution overview*

- A marketing concept

- Confidence in their process

...will almost always attract funding faster than the filmmaker who simply shows up with enthusiasm and a script.

Film is an art.

Funding is a business.

To succeed in the business, you must present yourself as someone worth partnering with.

MOVIES ARE A BUSINESS: AND FUNDING PARTNERS SEE THEM AS SUCH - YOU WILL NEED TO DO THE SAME.

We cannot emphasize this enough:

Funding partners expect you to treat your film like a business.

That doesn't mean you sacrifice creativity.

It means you support creativity with structure.

Filmmaking is:

- Project Management

- Leadership

- Budgeting

- Scheduling

- Communication

- Negotiation

- Relationship-Building

- Risk Mitigation

The more you understand this, the easier funding becomes.

Funding partners want to know you respect the process, understand the industry, and can deliver what you promise.

MONEY IS ALWAYS AVAILABLE FOR GREAT PROJECTS

One of the greatest lies in filmmaking is "there's no money."

There is *always* money.

The real question—the only question—is:

"How can I make my project great, and how can I communicate that greatness so others believe in it too?"

Greatness doesn't mean perfection.

It means clarity.

A project becomes fundable when:

- The concept is clear

- The message is meaningful

- *The audience is identifiable*

- *The filmmaker is believable*

- *The execution plan is logical*

- *The benefits to the funding partner are obvious*

- *The passion is contagious*

Money flows to preparation.

Money flows to clarity.

Money flows to confidence.

Money flows to vision.

If your project is truly great, and you can express that greatness effectively, funding will find you.

25 Questions Filmmakers Should Ask

1. What makes my project worth funding?

2. Does my film have a clear, meaningful purpose?

3. Who would benefit emotionally, socially, or professionally from supporting my film?

4. How strong is my creative vision, and can I communicate it clearly?

5. Do I understand the value my film offers to potential partners?

6. Am I thinking about funding as a business activity?

7. Have I prepared professional materials that demonstrate credibility?

8. What level of funding does my project realistically require?

9. How would more funding improve my production?

10. What compromises might low funding force me into?

11. Why would someone want to support my film besides financial return?

12. Do I have a plan for distribution and visibility?

13. What makes me fundable as a filmmaker?

14. How well do I understand the psychology of funding partners?

15. What emotional reasons might someone have to participate in my film?

16. What logical reasons might someone have to participate?

17. How prepared am I to answer tough questions about budget and execution?

18. Do I believe in my project strongly enough to ask others to believe in it?

19. What relationships could I begin building right now that may lead to funding?

20. What level of confidence do I project when discussing my film?

21. How can I make my project feel "great" in the eyes of others?

22. Does my project stand out in a crowded marketplace?

23. Am I prepared to treat my film like a business venture?

24. What proof can I show that I am capable of delivering on my promises?

25. What is the very next step I must take to move this project closer to funding?

How To Use These Ideas To Create Funding For Your Film

Below are practical steps you can take immediately.

1. Strengthen Your Project Concept Until It Is Clearly "Great"

Ask yourself:

- What makes this film unique?

- Why does it matter?

- *Why now?*

- *Who cares?*

A project becomes fundable when it is meaningful and easy to understand.

2. Create Improved Presentation Materials

Develop:

- *A clear one-page summary*

- *A simple pitch deck*

- *A concise verbal pitch*

- *A believable, transparent budget*

These tools show you are prepared and serious.

3. Identify Non-Financial Motivations for Support

Most partners don't support films for money, they support:

- *Personal Causes*

- *Professional Alignment*

- *Legacy*

- *Impact*

- *Visibility*

- *Identity*

- *Emotion*

Identify these motivations early.

4. Build Relationships Before Asking for Money

Reach out to:

- *Community Leaders*

- *Organizations*

- *Brands*

- *Individuals*

- *Arts groups*

- *Businesses*

Relationships build trust.

Trust builds funding.

5. Position Yourself as a Confident Creative Professional

People fund filmmakers who:

- *Communicate with clarity*

- *Understand their business*

- *Show leadership qualities*

- *Display organization*

- *Exhibit passion without desperation*

Your demeanor is part of your pitch.

6. Show That Your Film Has Reach and Value

Money flows to visibility.

Demonstrate:

- *Your audience*

- *Your distribution approach*

- *Your marketing ideas*

- *Your community connections*

- *Your plan for impact*

Even a simple outreach plan increases your credibility.

7. Treat Funding as a Skill, Not a Mystery

Rehearse your pitch.

Refine your budget.

Practice conversations.

Prepare answers to common questions.

Study the psychology of partners.

Skills grow with repetition.

Chapter 3

WHAT KIND OF FUNDING ARE YOU SEEKING?

Funding isn't "one-size-fits-all." Before you ask anyone for a penny, you need clarity on exactly what kind of funding your film requires, who it makes sense to approach, and how your project fits into the broader ecosystem of film financing. Most filmmakers skip this step, they chase money without understanding what they're actually chasing. That always ends the same way: no money.

Your film's genre, scope, length, style, cast, distribution plan, and creative ambition will determine how much funding you need, what kind of funding will serve you best, and what types of partners you should be seeking.

If you're making a character-driven drama with two actors and one location, you don't need the same amount—or the same type—of funding as someone mounting a creature-feature with VFX. And if you're seeking $250K, the people you approach will be vastly different than if you're seeking $10 million. The more clarity you have, the more confident you will be, and confidence converts investors.

Another overlooked step: *How did you arrive at the budget?* Can you show that each number is grounded in reality? As an investor, nothing is more alarming than a filmmaker who "thinks" they need $800K but can't explain why. Investors don't invest in guesswork—they invest in preparedness.

Remember, **money always has a cost.** Whether it's equity (giving away ownership), debt (paying back interest), partnerships (sharing control), or crowdfunding (delivering rewards and perks), each form of funding changes the nature of your film and your responsibilities. Not every funding source is healthy. Not every money partner is good for the long-term of your career. Some will support your vision—others will smother it.

Funding is also a relationship. The right funding partner elevates the film. The wrong one can sink it before production even begins. Choose wisely.

If you want funding, you must know:

- What kind of film you're making?

- What level of funding it requires?

- Who is best suited to provide it?

- What the cost of the money is?

- And whether that relationship will help or harm your film.

Get clear, get specific, and get strategic, because clarity attracts capital.

25 Important Questions Filmmakers Should Ask

These questions help filmmakers refine their funding strategy, identify gaps, and become more fundable.

A. Project & Vision Clarity

1. *What genre is my film, and how does that impact the budget size?*

2. *What is the film's intended length and style, and what does that realistically cost?*

3. *What cast level am I targeting, and what budget implications does that create?*

4. *Have I created a line-item budget that accurately reflects industry realities?*

5. *What makes my project unique or marketable compared to similar films?*

6. *Why would someone want to invest in this film versus thousands of others?*

B. Budget & Financial Strategy

7. *How much money do I actually need, and how did I calculate that?*

8. *Is there flexibility in my budget? What's the minimum viable budget?*

9. *Does my budget include marketing, publicity, deliverables, and distribution costs?*

10. *Have I researched comparable films and their budgets to justify my ask?*

11. *What is my plan for profitability, and can I communicate it simply?*

12. *How fast do I need the money, and is that realistic based on my strategy?*

C. Funding Sources

13. *Which funding sources best align with my film (equity investors, lenders, grants, crowdfunding, partnerships, institutional money, etc·)?*

14. *What are the pros and cons of each funding source for this specific project?*

15. *What is the cost of each type of money (equity percentages, interest rates, backend points, creative control, etc·)?*

16. *Which of these funding options best supports long-term relationships and future films?*

17. *Which funding options should I avoid because they may hinder the project?*

D. Investor Relations

18. *Who is the ideal investor for this film?*

19. *What do they want in exchange—money, prestige, involvement, creative credit, association?*

20. *Can I clearly express why this film is a strong opportunity?*

21. *Can I clearly communicate the risks honestly while maintaining confidence?*

22. *How will the investor get their money back, and how soon?*

E. Practical Execution

23. *Do I have the materials (pitch deck, business plan, lookbook, schedule, comps) ready to show credibility?*

24. *How will I present the budget in a way that feels professional and trustworthy?*

25. *Am I prepared to answer difficult questions about the budget, cast, risks, and profitability?*

Suggestions & Ideas: How to Use These Concepts to Secure Funding for Your Film

Here is how you can turn this knowledge into action:

1. Build a Funding Profile for Your Film

Create a one-page document that outlines:

- *What type of film you're making?*

- *Exact budget range*

- *Funding sources you plan to pursue*

- *Why this film is financially viable*

- *What makes you credible*

This becomes your internal compass and keeps you from wasting time on mismatched funding sources.

2. Use Genre and Scope to Target the Right Funders

Different funders respond to different genres:

- *Horror: private investors, equity funds, angel investors*

- *Documentaries: grants, social-purpose organizations, corporate partners*

- *Rom-coms or dramedies: equity investors, soft money, small funds*

- *Action or thriller: international pre-sales, co-productions*

Match the film to the money.

3. Create Tiered Budget Options

Show investors you are flexible and prepared:

- *Budget A (ideal vision)*

- *Budget B (lean version)*

- *Budget C (micro-budget "guaranteed shoot" version)*

Investors love filmmakers who can adapt without compromising quality.

4. Calculate the Cost of Money Before You Accept It

- *Equity means giving away ownership*

- *Debt means repayment regardless of performance*

- *Partnerships mean shared control*

- *Crowdfunding means delivering rewards*

A filmmaker who knows the "cost of money" appears seasoned and trustworthy.

5. Use Your Uniqueness as a Funding Magnet

Ask:

- *What personal credibility do you have?*

- *What unique access (locations, communities, experts, cast) do you bring?*

- *What makes this project culturally timely or commercially relevant?*

Your uniqueness is your selling point—highlight it relentlessly.

6. Build a Clear Funding Timeline

Most filmmakers fall apart here.

Break your fundraising into phases:

- *Phase 1: Development money (decks, casting, legal)*

- *Phase 2: Early equity/soft money committed*

- *Phase 3: Main investors + pre-sales*

- *Phase 4: Gap financing and finishing funds*

A timeline builds investor confidence·

7. Approach the Right People at the Right Stage

For example:

- *Crowdfunding first*

- *Then private investors*

- *Then partnerships*

- *Then lenders (only once major money is in place)*

Each step increases credibility and reduces risk·

8. Present Your Budget With Authority

Show:

- *Where the money goes*

- *How efficiently you'll use it*

- *How it connects to the screen value*

- *How it helps generate returns*

A filmmaker who understands money attracts money.

9. Build Long-Term Funding Relationships

Investors don't just invest in a film—they invest in the filmmaker.

Treat every connection as a future partnership.

10. Make Your Project Great

This is the heart of the section:

"Money is always available for great projects."

Ask:

- *What can you do to strengthen the concept?*

- *Can you attach a recognizable/bankable actor?*

- *Can you secure a unique location?*

- *Can you line up pre-distribution partners?*

Every improvement increases fundability.

It's also important to ask your potential film funding partner what are the elements that will be most important to them. Most filmmakers do not involve potential film funding partners in these processes. Involving them early without asking them for money is a smart way to understand how they will be thinking about your project when you do ask them for money.

And even if they aren't the ones who will ultimately be funding your film, they will give you some very powerful insights into how money people think about projects like yours.

Chapter 4

WHAT KIND OF FUNDING ARE YOU SEEKING - PART 2

After reading what I shared in the last section, I decided I needed to give you more. This is such an essential question that you need to answer in order to be successful in acquiring your funding. Let's go into greater detail and explore a few more thoughts to help you be more prepared for questions that will arise from your potential film funding partners.

Every filmmaker reaches a point where the dream of making a movie collides with the practical reality of financing it. But before you even start looking for money, you need to know exactly what kind of funding you're seeking.

This isn't just about numbers; it's about understanding your project, its scope, and the people who will ultimately be part of your film's financial journey.

Too often, filmmakers ask for money without clarity. They know they need a budget, but they haven't considered *how much*, *what type*, or *why that type fits their project*. They focus on asking for funding and forget the critical step: defining the funding need in the first place.

This chapter is about creating that clarity, because the way you define your funding need will determine:

- Who you can approach,

- How you present your project,

- The type of funding that will best serve your film,

- And how sustainable your relationships with funders will be.

Funding isn't just a transaction—it's a relationship. And every relationship begins with clarity.

1. Understanding Your Project

Before asking for a single dollar, you need to dissect your film in terms of genre, length, style, and cast. These elements are not trivial—they influence every aspect of your funding strategy.

- ***Genre:*** *Investors, lenders, and partners evaluate projects differently depending on the genre. A horror film, for example, may attract private investors looking for high return potential with minimal production requirements. A documentary may appeal to social purpose organizations, educational grants, or foundations. Comedy or drama features may attract private investors with an interest in marketable commercial narratives. Your genre is a signaling tool* that tells potential funders whether your project aligns with their goals.

- **Length:** The runtime of your film affects the budget, the complexity of production, and the type of funding you can realistically secure. Shorts may attract grants, small private donations, or crowdfunding, while features often require equity, co-production arrangements, or larger institutional investments.

- **Style:** The visual, narrative, and production style of your film informs the type of partners you should seek. High-concept or visually ambitious projects may require investors who understand the scope and are willing to take on the increased risk and cost. Simpler, character-driven stories may appeal to smaller, relationship-focused funders.

- **Cast:** A recognizable actor can open doors and attract specific funding partners. At the same time, a less-known cast may make your budget leaner but require other creative angles to convince funders of the project's value. Knowing how casting affects your production costs will help you define the amount you need and the type of funding partner most suited to your project.

Every element of your project is interconnected with the funding strategy. Your goal is to define these elements not just creatively, but strategically. Investors and funding partners are not just evaluating your idea—they are evaluating your plan, your preparedness, and the likelihood that their support will produce results.

2. Determining How Much Funding You Need

Once you've clarified your project's creative aspects, the next step is calculating the funding requirement. This is where many filmmakers stumble. They guess, overestimate, or underestimate, which erodes credibility.

A proper funding assessment should answer the following:

- *How much money are you seeking?*

This is your total production and operational cost. Include all production, post-production, and necessary administrative costs. You must have a line-item understanding of your budget and be able to justify every figure.

- *How soon do you need the funding?*

Timeline is critical. Some investors can commit quickly, while others need months or years of preparation. Your schedule should be realistic and align with the type of funding you're pursuing. Rushing funding without preparation can compromise your project and credibility.

- *How did you arrive at this budget?*

Funders will ask for detailed reasoning behind your numbers. They want to see logic, research, and transparency. Budgets based on estimates, gut feelings, or creative wish lists are red flags. Prepare to explain:

o Crew Costs

o Cast Fees

o Equipment Rentals

o Locations

o Post-Production

o Marketing And Distribution Costs

This is your opportunity to demonstrate professionalism and command of the business side of filmmaking.

● **Is there flexibility in your budget?**

Investors appreciate filmmakers who can adjust without sacrificing the integrity of the project. Flexibility shows problem-solving skills and preparedness. It also allows you to approach different funders with slightly different packages depending on their size, priorities, or preferred risk exposure.

- *Does your budget include marketing and other ancillary costs?*

Many filmmakers forget that funding is not only for making the film, but it's also for delivering the finished product to an audience. Marketing, festival submissions, distribution, and audience engagement costs must be included in your overall funding plan. A filmmaker who neglects this risks a partially complete project that fails to reach its potential.

3. What Makes Your Project and You Unique

Funding decisions are rarely made solely on the merits of the script. Investors and funding partners evaluate the people behind the project as much as the project itself.

- *Why should someone invest in this project over dozens of others?*

- *What credibility, experience, or passion do I bring to the table?*

- *What unique access do I have to cast, locations, or distribution opportunities?*

The uniqueness of your project, combined with your credibility as a filmmaker, is what attracts funding. A funder may pass on a mediocre project by a well-known director, but they will almost always consider a strong project with a filmmaker who demonstrates preparation, knowledge, and strategic thinking.

It's not just about your project—it's about *you* as the vehicle for that project's success.

4. Types of Funding

Once you understand your project, your budget, and your unique selling points, it's time to evaluate the types of funding available. Not all funding sources are created equal, and choosing the wrong type can compromise your film or your long-term relationships.

Crowdfunding

Crowdfunding can provide upfront cash while building an audience. It's ideal for short films, independent features, and socially-driven projects. Crowdfunding works best if you have:

- A compelling story

- A clear marketing strategy

- A network willing to support

- Tangible rewards or incentives

Crowdfunding also builds a community around your project, which can help with marketing and distribution later·

Funding Partners

Funding partners are individuals, organizations, or businesses that invest in your film because they believe in the vision or in you as a filmmaker·

They may not expect financial return but seek participation, association, or impact· This type of funding is often flexible and supportive of creative freedom, but choosing the right partner is essential· Not every relationship will benefit your project in the long term·

Investors

Equity investors expect financial return· They provide larger sums and may bring industry connections, but their involvement often comes with expectations: ownership stakes, decision-making influence, or deadlines· Carefully consider whether an investor's goals align with your creative vision.

Lenders

Lenders provide money that must be repaid, often with interest. While this can bridge funding gaps, it adds financial risk. Only take this route if your project has a clear path to revenue that can cover repayment obligations.

Institutional Money

Grants, foundations, and government programs may provide funding with few strings attached. The application process may be competitive, but successful applicants gain credibility, legitimacy, and access to networks of support.

5. Understanding the Cost of Money

Funding always comes at a cost. No source of money is free, and every option comes with trade-offs:

- **Equity:** *giving away a percentage of ownership in exchange for capital*

- **Debt:** *repaying principal plus interest, independent of project success*

- **Crowdfunding:** *fulfilling rewards or delivering perks to supporters*

- *Partnerships: potentially sharing control or credit*

A critical part of determining what funding to pursue is understanding the true cost of that money and whether it aligns with your long-term goals. Sometimes the cheapest money is not the best money. Relationships, creative control, and reputational impact are often more valuable than nominal savings.

6. Matching Funding Sources to Your Project and Goals

Every funding source has strengths and weaknesses. The most successful filmmakers take a strategic approach:

- **Short Films:** Crowdfunding, grants, small private contributions

- **Documentaries:** Institutional grants, foundations, educational partners, impact-driven donors

- **Feature Narratives:** Equity investors, co-productions, pre-sales, partnerships

- **High-Budget Projects:** Equity investors, co-productions, distribution guarantees

Ask yourself:

Which type of funding not only provides the money but also enhances your project through expertise, connections, or credibility?

Funding is not just transactional, it is relational. Choosing the right partners can make the difference between a smooth production and constant creative compromise.

7. Timing and Urgency

Not all funding needs are equal. How soon you need money should influence who you approach and how you structure your request. Rushed projects may require emergency loans or high-cost funding, while well-prepared projects can attract strategic investors or partners willing to commit over months of planning.

Being clear about your timeline also sets realistic expectations with funders. Those who know when you need funding—and why—perceive your project as organized, professional, and credible.

8. Strategic Questions for Filmmakers

To summarize the thinking behind this chapter, here are 25 questions every filmmaker should ask when considering what kind of funding to seek:

1.   What genre best describes my film?

2. *How does the genre affect the type of funding I can pursue?*

3. *What is the intended length of the project, and how does it affect my budget?*

4. *How does the production style influence potential funders?*

5. *What cast level am I aiming for, and what are the cost implications?*

6. *How much total funding do I realistically need?*

7. *How soon do I need the funds?*

8. *How did I calculate the budget, and can I justify each line item?*

9. *Is my budget flexible, and if so, where can adjustments be made?*

10. *Does the budget include marketing, distribution, and other essential costs?*

11. *What makes this project unique compared to others in the market?*

12. *What unique value do I, as a filmmaker, bring to the project?*

13. *Who would be the ideal funding partner for this type of project?*

14. *Should I pursue crowdfunding, investors, lenders, or institutional funding?*

15. *What is the cost of each type of funding for this project?*

16. *Which funding sources align best with my long-term goals?*

17. *Which funding sources could create creative or reputational conflicts?*

18. *How do I match the project's goals to the funder's interests?*

19. *Can I communicate the value of the project clearly to potential partners?*

20. *How will my timeline affect the type of funding I can realistically secure?*

21. *Which funding source will enhance rather than limit my creative freedom?*

22. *How can I demonstrate credibility and preparedness to funders?*

23. *What is my plan for repayment, return, or delivery of value to funders?*

24. *How can I structure funding relationships for long-term collaboration?*

25. *How will each funding decision affect the future of my career and future projects?*

9 Practical Applications: Using This Chapter to Fund Your Film

Here's how to put this knowledge into action:

1. *Define your project completely:* Genre, style, length, cast, and production scope must all be clearly articulated.

2. *Create a detailed, line-item budget:* Include production, post, marketing, and distribution costs.

3. *Determine the cost of money:* Understand the implications of each type of funding.

4. *Map funding sources to your project type:* Identify the sources most aligned with your genre, timeline, and budget.

5. *Evaluate relationships:* Choose funding partners who align with your creative vision and long-term goals.

6. *Establish flexibility:* Create tiered budget options and alternative funding strategies.

7. *Prepare a funding timeline:* Show funders when money is needed and why, and how it will be used.

8. *Highlight your uniqueness:* Emphasize both the project's originality and your credibility as a filmmaker.

9. *Communicate clearly and confidently:* Build a professional narrative around your funding ask.

10. *Strategically sequence funding approaches:* Use crowdfunding, grants, investors, and partners in the optimal order for success.

By approaching funding strategically, you stop chasing money blindly and instead attract the right partners at the right time, building relationships that benefit both your project and your career.

Chapter 5

PREPARING FOR FUNDING

The stage of preparation is the most critical, yet often most overlooked, aspect of film funding. Many filmmakers assume that if they have a good script or a passionate pitch, money will follow. That assumption is not only misguided, but it is also why so many projects stall before production ever begins. Preparing effectively for funding is not just a matter of creating materials; it is about building credibility, trust, and clarity in the eyes of potential film funding partners.

In this chapter, we will focus on the steps and strategies that allow filmmakers to present themselves as organized, professional, and reliable—qualities that attract funding. Preparation is where you transform your film from an idea into an opportunity that money people can understand, evaluate, and support.

1. Building a Pitch Deck with the Money Person in Mind

The first step in preparing for funding is creating a **pitch deck**, but not the kind most filmmakers think of. Too often, filmmakers design decks to showcase the story, characters, and their own artistic vision. While these elements are important, they do not answer the questions that funding partners care about most.

What money people want to know:

- *Your experience and past successes:* Have you completed projects before? What is your track record of delivery and credibility?

- *How the money will come back:* What is the return on investment, or what value does supporting your film bring?

- **Risk mitigation:** How are you minimizing potential losses or problems in production?

- **Timeline:** How long will the project take to produce and deliver?

- **Contingency plans:** What happens if things don't go as planned?

A pitch deck focused on the filmmaker's ego will rarely succeed. A pitch deck designed from the **money person's perspective** answers their questions, reduces uncertainty, and positions the filmmaker as capable and trustworthy.

Elements to include:

- Executive summary of the project

- Short bio emphasizing credibility and track record

- Budget overview with transparency on how funds will be used

- Marketing, distribution, and monetization plan

- Timeline with key milestones

- Risk analysis and mitigation strategies

- Potential rewards or value for the funding partner

Remember:

The deck is not about impressing your friends or showcasing your creativity; it's about building confidence in a potential funder.

2. Building Effective Pitch Materials

Beyond the pitch deck, the materials you prepare for potential funders must answer the deeper, practical questions they have. These materials become your foundation for all discussions and help establish your credibility.

Key materials to prepare:

- *Past successes and experience: Have you delivered projects successfully in the past? Highlight relevant projects and results.*

- *Financial plan: Detail exactly how the money will be spent, how it will generate returns, and how it contributes to profitability.*

- *Risk mitigation plan: Identify potential risks and your strategies to address them. This can include backup locations, alternate talent, production insurance, and contingency budgeting.*

- *Timeline and milestones: Show a clear, realistic schedule from pre-production through post-production, marketing, and distribution.*

- *Fallback plan: Explain what happens if the project doesn't succeed as expected and how partners' interests will be protected.*

These materials should not be overwhelming, but they should be thorough and precise. Money partners are looking for clarity and assurance, not artistic flair.

3. Having a Company

One of the most overlooked aspects of preparation is the legal and organizational structure of your project.

Filmmakers often underestimate the importance of having a formal company through which funds can flow. The company structure communicates professionalism and provides legal clarity for both you and the funding partner.

At one of the Film Funding events I was involved with a few years ago, I decided to ask a question of one of the filmmakers to teach a lesson to the group. I asked this filmmaker if I was going to cut a check for a million dollars for his project, to who should I make it out to.

His answer was to make it out to him personally.

Can you see the problem with this? No potential film funding partner has ever cut a check to an individual for their film. (Unless they were a relative) Think it through:

— *A check to a personal account means you are commingling their funds with your life.*

— *A check to a personal account is going to automatically be taxed at a much higher rate, which means a significant amount of their investment is immediately going to disappear to the IRS.*

— *It tells the potential film funding partner now knows that you are not thinking about this venture as a business.*

Questions to address about your company:

• *What kind of company structure works best for this project (LLC, corporation, partnership)?*

- *Will the potential film funding partner be a formal partner in the company?*

- *What powers or decision-making authority will they have?*

- *How are responsibilities and risk shared between the filmmaker and funding partners?*

- *What legal protections exist for both parties?*

Having a company not only streamlines the financial process but also signals that you are serious and prepared. It reduces uncertainty, creates clarity around roles and responsibilities, and protects all parties involved.

A company structure also makes it easier to attract multiple funding partners without confusion or conflict.

4. Setting Up Meetings

Once your pitch deck and materials are in place, preparation shifts to the logistics of meetings with potential film funding partners. The way you approach meetings can dramatically influence whether a funding conversation progresses.

Key considerations:

- *Who should be present:* Include only those directly relevant to the discussion. You may need a producer, legal counsel, or financial advisor in addition to yourself. Too many people can confuse the conversation; too few can reduce credibility.

- *How many meetings will it take?* Rarely is a single meeting sufficient. Most funding relationships require multiple conversations to build trust, clarify questions, and refine proposals. Be prepared for lots of meetings and understand that you will get better at pitching with every meeting you take.

- *Timing and expectations:* Ask the potential partner how much time they need to make a decision and *what information will be critical to their evaluation. This allows you to tailor follow-ups and avoid unnecessary pressure.*

- ***Preparation for objections:*** *Anticipate questions and objections about budget, risks, timeline, and contingencies. Being ready with clear, concise answers builds confidence and demonstrates experience.*

Remember: *funding is a relationship, not a transaction. Each meeting is part of a process of building trust, credibility, and alignment.*

5. The Money Is in the Follow-Up

One of the most critical lessons in funding is that wanting and receiving are not the same. Rarely does a potential funder commit immediately after the first meeting. In my experience, only once in my career did a funder commit immediately on the first discussion. Most funding relationships require careful follow-up.

Effective Follow-Up Strategies:

- *Send a personalized summary of the discussion, reiterating the project's value and addressing any concerns raised.*

- *Provide additional documentation if requested, such as revised budgets, schedules, or risk mitigation strategies.*

- *Maintain consistent communication without being pushy—demonstrate persistence, professionalism, and commitment.*

- *Update partners on progress and milestones, even before they commit. This signals momentum and professionalism.*

Follow-up is not just about reminding someone to make a decision. It is about demonstrating that you are organized, responsive, and serious about delivering results.

6. Learning from Observing Others

Hosting events like the speed pitching event at the AFC revealed a recurring pattern: many filmmakers are not prepared to discuss their projects from a business perspective. They focus on creativity but neglect the practical questions that funders care about.

Key takeaways from observing others:

- *Funders want clarity, transparency, and professionalism.*

- *Creativity alone will not secure funding.*

- *The ability to answer business-oriented questions differentiates fundable filmmakers from the rest.*

- *Preparation signals credibility and reduces perceived risk.*

Preparation is not just about materials, it is a mindset. Being able to switch from a creative to a business perspective is essential for attracting the right partners.

7. Funding Is Drawn in Two Main Phases

*Preparation affects **two key stages** of funding:*

1. ***Initial funding to make and market the film:** This includes raising the money needed for production, post-production, and initial marketing efforts. Being prepared ensures you can secure these funds efficiently and responsibly.*

2. ***Funding during audience engagement:** Once the film is made, additional funding may be required for marketing campaigns, ticket sales, and rewards for funding partners. Well-prepared filmmakers create a plan to attract funds at this stage as well, ensuring the film reaches its audience effectively.*

The same principles apply at both stages: clarity, preparedness, credibility, and relationship-building.

8. Preparation Is Determined by Who You Are

A significant portion of a funding decision is based on you as a filmmaker. Money partners evaluate not just the project, but your experience, reputation, and relationships.

Consider:

- Your preparedness: Have you completed projects, built budgets, and organized your pitch materials?

- Your track record: Have you successfully delivered films in the past?

- Your network: Who are you working with, and what experience do they bring?

- Your reputation: How are you perceived in the industry, both creatively and professionally?

Funders are investing in people, not just ideas. Your credibility, experience, and professionalism can make the difference between securing funding and being passed over.

25 Key Questions Filmmakers Should Ask About Preparation

1. Have I built a pitch deck designed for the funder, not for myself?

2. Does my deck answer questions about risk, returns, and timeline?

3. Have I clearly documented past successes and experience?

4. Does my budget demonstrate realistic planning and contingencies?

5. Have I identified risk mitigation strategies?

6. Have I included a timeline with milestones for production, marketing, and delivery?

7. *Do I have contingency plans for things that may go wrong?*

8. *Have I structured a company for the project, and is it clear to funders?*

9. *If the funder becomes a partner, what powers or influence will they have?*

10. *Who should attend meetings to maximize credibility and clarity?*

11. *How many meetings will it take to secure funding?*

12. *What information will be critical to a funder's decision?*

13. *How soon can a funder make a decision?*

14. *Have I prepared answers to common objections about the project?*

15. *Am I ready to discuss the project from a business perspective, not just creative?*

16. *Do I have a follow-up plan after initial meetings?*

17. *How will I maintain momentum and trust during follow-up?*

18. *What lessons can I learn from observing other filmmakers' preparation?*

19. *How does my preparation signal credibility and reduce perceived risk?*

20. *Have I planned for funding beyond the production stage?*

21. *How will I attract additional funds during audience engagement and distribution?*

22. *How does my track record influence funding decisions?*

23. *Who are my key collaborators, and how does their experience add credibility?*

24. *What is my reputation in the industry, and how can I demonstrate it to funders?*

25. *How will I continuously improve my preparation to secure funding for future projects?*

Practical Suggestions: Using Preparation to Attract Funding

1. ***Design pitch materials for the funder:*** *Focus on risk, returns, timeline, and credibility—not just your creative vision.*

2. ***Document past successes clearly:*** *Include examples of completed projects, results, and lessons learned.*

3. ***Create a detailed, line-item budget:*** *Include production, post-production, marketing, and contingency costs.*

4. ***Set up a company structure:*** *Clarify ownership, partnership roles, and responsibilities.*

5. ***Plan meetings strategically:*** *Know who should attend, how many meetings are needed, and what information funders require.*

6. **Prepare for follow-up:** Anticipate questions and provide updates or additional information without being pushy.

7. **Develop a business mindset:** Switch between creative storytelling and clear business communication.

8. **Plan for funding in two phases:** Initial production funding and audience/distribution funding.

9. **Highlight your credibility and network:** Show funders why you and your team are capable of delivering results.

10. **Iterate and refine preparation:** Continuously improve pitch materials, company structure, and follow-up strategies for current and future projects.

By mastering preparation, you not only increase your chances of securing funding but also lay the groundwork for long-term success. A well-prepared filmmaker signals professionalism, reduces perceived risk, and positions themselves as a reliable partner. Every meeting, pitch, and follow-up is an opportunity to demonstrate that your film is worth supporting and that you are the filmmaker capable of delivering it.

Chapter 6

WHO HAS YOUR MONEY?

One of the most fundamental questions every filmmaker must answer is: who has the money, and why would they give it to you? Many filmmakers make assumptions about funding sources—they assume someone won't participate, that they don't have money, or that they aren't interested. The reality is almost always different. You will often be surprised by who is willing to invest, support, or contribute to your project if you take the time to identify potential film funding partners correctly. This chapter is about mapping out your potential funders, understanding their motivations, and preparing yourself to approach them strategically. Money does not exist in a vacuum, it comes from people. Understanding people, their goals, and their resources is the key to successful film funding.

1. Money Can Come from More Than One Source

It is rare that a single source provides the full budget for a film. Even large studio projects often combine financing from multiple avenues. The same principle applies to independent films. Your funding may come from:

- Individual investors

- Institutional investors

- Lenders

- Philanthropists

- Crowdfunding platforms and fans

- Sponsorship and product placement deals

Each source has unique expectations, motivations, and conditions. Recognizing this early allows you to approach fundraising strategically, rather than relying on hope or assumption.

A good exercise is to start with people you know.

Make a list of everyone in your network who may be willing to hear about your project. This includes friends, family, colleagues, mentors, or anyone who might have access to additional resources. Even if they cannot provide funding themselves, they may know someone who can. The power of networking cannot be overstated: people are more likely to trust introductions from those they already know and respect.

2. Exercise: Map Your Network

Before you can approach funding partners effectively, it's important to think critically about your network:

- Who do you know that might be willing to hear about your project?

- *What is their lifestyle, interests, and resources?*

- *Where do they spend their time?*

- *What causes or projects do they already support?*

- *Who else do they know who might be interested in participating?*

By creating a map of potential partners, you not only identify people to approach directly, but you also uncover indirect connections that could significantly expand your funding reach. The key is to be intentional: most filmmakers fail to put effort into thinking through who their potential funders are, and who those funders may know.

3. Understanding Different Kinds of Film Funding Partners

Potential film funding partners are diverse. They are motivated by different goals, and they provide funding in various ways.

Understanding these categories allows you to tailor your approach to the person you are speaking with, rather than using a generic pitch.

A. Vanity Investors

Vanity investors are individuals who contribute to your project primarily for personal reasons: visibility, participation, or recognition. This could include:

- *Aspiring actors who want to appear in a film*

- *Professionals who want a film credit for career advancement*

- *Individuals who wish to fulfill a lifelong dream of participating in a film*

- *Those seeking prestige or status among family, friends, or social circles*

Vanity investors are motivated by personal gain or satisfaction, not necessarily financial return. Approaching them requires understanding what drives them and connecting your project to their personal goals.

B. Institutional Investors

Institutional investors operate more formally. They usually have a structured process for evaluating whether they can or will invest.

Typically, these investors are seeking equity ownership or financial return. Institutional investors may include:

- Investment funds

- Private equity groups

- Film financing companies

When approaching institutional investors, preparation is critical.

They will scrutinize budgets, projections, legal structures, and risk mitigation plans. A clear, professional, and credible presentation is essential.

C. Lenders

Lenders provide temporary financing that must be repaid, often with interest.

They usually require security or collateral. While debt financing can be effective, it comes with risk:

- *Penalties may apply for late repayment*

- *Interest adds cost to the project*

- *Failure to repay can damage your reputation or legal standing*

The advantage is that once the debt is repaid, you no longer have obligations to the lender. For filmmakers, this can be an attractive way to fund specific aspects of a project without giving away equity or creative control.

D. Philanthropists

Philanthropic funding comes from individuals or organizations motivated by causes or passions. These funders may contribute because they believe in the cultural, social, or artistic significance of your project. Approaching philanthropists requires:

- Identifying shared values or interests

- Demonstrating the impact of your film beyond financial return

- Connecting your project to a cause that matters to them

Philanthropists are often flexible, supportive, and motivated by purpose rather than profit.

E. Crowdfunding and Fans

Crowdfunding leverages the enthusiasm of fans or a community that believes in your project. It is particularly effective for projects with:

- Pre-existing audiences

- A compelling story or cause

- *Tangible rewards for supporters*

Crowdfunding not only generates money but also builds an engaged audience, which can later support ticket sales, merchandise, or promotional campaigns.

F. Sponsorship and Product Placement

Some funders are motivated by marketing opportunities. Brands, corporations, and organizations may contribute funds in exchange for:

- *Product exposure in the film*

- *Affiliation with a specific audience or demographic*

- *Association with a successful or culturally relevant project*

Sponsorship and product placement can be highly strategic, providing not just money but also visibility, credibility, and potential partnerships for future projects.

4. Understanding Motivations of Funding Partners

One of the most critical lessons in funding is that money comes from people, and people have different motivations. Successful filmmakers recognize this and tailor their approach accordingly. Not every funder will be motivated by the same thing:

- Vanity investors seek recognition or participation

- Institutional investors seek financial return and equity

- Lenders seek repayment and security

- Philanthropists seek impact and alignment with values

- Fans and crowdfunding contributors seek connection, excitement, or perks

- Sponsors seek marketing value and audience engagement

Understanding motivations allows you to craft a message that resonates with each potential partner.

A one-size-fits-all pitch rarely works. Each conversation should reflect the funder's unique goals.

5. Who Qualifies as a Potential Film Funding Partner?

A person or organization is considered a potential film funding partner if they meet three criteria:

1. **They have the money:** *The first and most obvious requirement.*

2. **They have the desire:** *Motivation to participate is essential. Without it, even wealthy individuals are unlikely to contribute.*

3. **They have the ability to say yes:** *Influence, authority, and decision-making power are crucial. Approaching someone who cannot approve funding is a wasted effort.*

Identifying potential partners requires research, networking, and careful assessment of each individual's resources, interests, and capacity to contribute.

6. Avoiding Assumptions

Filmmakers often make assumptions that hinder fundraising success. These assumptions include:

- *This person doesn't have money, so they can't help."*

- *"This person would never be interested in my project."*

- *Only industry professionals can contribute."*

The reality is that potential funders can come from unexpected places, including people you know casually, fans, local businesses, or philanthropists connected to causes your film aligns with.

Avoid assumptions and remain open to exploring possibilities. Often, the most surprising funders become your strongest supporters.

7. Building a List of Potential Funding Partners

Creating a list of potential funders is both practical and strategic. A structured approach includes:

1. **Personal network:** Friends, family, colleagues, mentors.

2. **Extended network:** Contacts of your contacts, professional associations, alumni groups, and local community leaders.

3. **Industry Contacts:** Producers, distributors, other filmmakers, agents.

4. **Corporations and brands:** Potential sponsors or product placement opportunities.

5. **Philanthropic organizations:** Foundations and individuals with interests aligned with your project.

6. **Fans and Community Supporters:** Social media followers, crowdfunding communities, and niche audience groups.

Once your list is created, segment it by type of funding partner, their likely motivations, and your strategy for approaching them·

Questions Filmmakers Should Ask

Here are 25 essential questions to guide filmmakers in identifying and understanding their funding partners:

1. *Who do I know personally that might be interested in my project?*

2. *Who do I know indirectly that might be willing to connect me with potential funders?*

3. *What motivates each potential funder (vanity, philanthropy, investment, marketing)?*

4. *Does this person or organization have the financial capacity to contribute meaningfully?*

5. *Do they have the authority to approve or commit funds?*

6. *What do they care about personally or professionally?*

7. *How does my project align with their goals or values?*

8. *Have I approached similar people in the past successfully?*

9. *Are they likely to respond to direct outreach, or is an introduction necessary?*

10. *What type of funding would this person or organization provide (equity, donation, sponsorship, loan)?*

11. *Are there risks associated with this partner (creative conflict, repayment issues, brand misalignment)?*

12. *How much time do they need to make a decision?*

13. *What information will be most important to them in evaluating the project?*

14. *Are there social, professional, or industry networks they are part of that I can access?*

15. *How should I communicate my pitch to resonate with their motivation?*

16. *Do they have a history of funding similar projects?*

17. *Are they looking for personal participation, such as acting or credit?*

18. *How do I demonstrate credibility and trustworthiness to them?*

19. *What is the potential upside for this funder?*

20. *What type of recognition or reward might they expect?*

21. *Are they a one-time funder or could they participate in multiple projects?*

22. *How do they prefer to receive updates or progress reports?*

23. *Are there other people they might recommend I approach?*

24. *What objections might they raise, and how can I address them?*

25. *How can I maintain a positive relationship even if they decline?*

8 Practical Suggestions and Ideas for Securing Funding

Here are actionable steps you can take based on this chapter:

1. ***Map your network:*** *Create a detailed list of everyone you know, categorize them by potential role, and consider who they might connect you with.*

2. ***Segment your potential partners:*** *Identify vanity investors, philanthropists, lenders, institutional investors, fans, and sponsors. Tailor your pitch to each group.*

3. ***Research thoroughly:*** *Understand their motivations, history of support, and capacity to contribute.*

4. **Craft personalized outreach:** Connect your project to their goals, values, or desires.

5. **Leverage introductions:** Ask potential partners who else they know that might be interested in supporting your project.

6. **Avoid assumptions:** Treat every potential partner as a real possibility until proven otherwise.

7. **Prioritize follow-up:** Maintain consistent communication, updates, and relationship-building.

8. **Demonstrate credibility:** Highlight past work, experience, and preparation to build confidence.

9. **Combine funding sources:** Use multiple channels strategically to meet your full budget.

10. **Maintain professionalism:** Every interaction signals your capacity to deliver the project successfully.

By understanding who has the money, why they might give it to you, and how to approach them strategically, you position your project for the highest likelihood of funding success.

The key is clarity, preparation, and relationship-building—money follows people who demonstrate credibility, value, and alignment with their motivations.

Chapter 7

WHERE TO FIND POTENTIAL FUNDING PARTNERS

Finding the right funding for your film is as much about research and strategy as it is about your creative idea. Too often, filmmakers struggle not because funding isn't available, but because they don't know where to look, or they fail to put in the effort to truly understand who potential funders are.

Money is not randomly distributed; it follows people who see value in your project, in you as a filmmaker, and in the opportunities your film creates. To secure funding, you need a systematic approach to identifying, qualifying, and connecting with potential film funding partners.

This chapter focuses on where to find potential film funding partners, how to locate individuals or institutions who could support your project, and how to qualify these potential partners before engaging with them.

If you don't have any idea of who you are looking for, chances are very good that you won't find them.

1. Building a Potential Film Funding Partner Profile

Before you start looking for funding, it's essential to develop a potential film funding partner profile. This is essentially a blueprint of the type of people or organizations who are most likely to invest in your project. The more you know about these people, the easier it becomes to find them and connect effectively.

A potential film funding profile should include:

- *Financial capacity:* Do they have the resources to support your project?

- ***Motivation:*** *Are they vanity investors, institutional investors, lenders, philanthropists, fans, or sponsors? What drives them to fund projects?*

- ***Influence:*** *Can they say yes? Do they have the authority to make financial decisions?*

- ***Interest alignment:*** *Does your project align with their personal or professional goals, passions, or values?*

- ***Network potential:*** *Who else do they know that might be interested in participating?*

Most filmmakers overlook this step, which leads to wasted effort approaching individuals who are either not qualified, not motivated, or not reachable. The more detailed your funding profile, the more efficient and effective your fundraising efforts will be.

2. Institutional Money Is Often Easiest to Locate

Institutional investors, such as film financing companies, private equity groups, or formalized investment funds, are typically easier to locate than individual investors. This is because they operate through formal channels and have an established presence in the market.

Tips for finding institutional money:

- *Research online directories of film investment funds and financing companies.*

- *Network with producers and filmmakers who have previously secured institutional funding.*

- *Attend industry events and conferences where institutional investors participate.*

- *Utilize professional associations and film commissions, which often maintain lists of potential funding organizations.*

Institutional investors have clear criteria for investment, which can make your approach more straightforward once you understand their requirements.

HINT: In some of our trainings, I share my personalized list of all the institutional money resources I have identified over the years. We call this The Money List. While you can get mine at these events, I would encourage you to start building your own right now. Start by recording any organization that has expressed interest in considering your project for funding. Be sure to include their name, contact information, the types of projects they are looking for, the amount of money they would potential contribute and notes you may have about terms and conditions they need or what they are specifically what kinds of projects they looking to get involved in. Then be sure to keep in touch with these people and build a relationship with them. It's always best to build a relationship with them so that when you need them, you're not just showing up with your hand out.

3. Friends and Family

Friends and family are a common starting point for many filmmakers. While this funding is often smaller in scale, it is immediate, accessible, and less formalized. Approaching friends and family successfully requires clarity and professionalism:

- Treat it like a business proposition, not a personal favor.

- Present your pitch materials, budget, and risk mitigation plans.

- Be clear about what they are contributing, what they can expect, and how it will be used.

- *Set expectations about returns or recognition, if applicable.*

Even if your friends or family cannot provide the full budget, they may know others who can, expanding your network further.

HINT: Always remember that friends and family are people whom you will have to see all throughout your life. Make sure you are honest and upfront with everyone about your projects, but especially these people. If there is a problem somewhere along the way, be sure to communicate quickly and honestly with them. Most challenges can be dealt with if you are clear and upfront.

4. Finding Individual Investors

Individual investors can range from experienced financiers to local business owners or professionals seeking creative opportunities. Unlike institutional money, individuals may be more flexible, motivated by personal interests or connections.

Tips for Approaching Individual Investors:

- *Identify professionals in industries you have access to or relationships with.*

- *Attend local networking events, trade shows, or industry gatherings.*

- *Prepare a tailored pitch that highlights both creative and business aspects.*

- *Understand their motivations, vanity, financial return, or personal interest.*

The key is to personalize your approach. Each investor is different, and one generic pitch is unlikely to resonate with everyone.

5. Vanity Players and Crowdfunding

Vanity investors, often motivated by recognition, participation, or personal satisfaction, can be a unique and valuable source of funding. Crowdfunding platforms like Kickstarter, Indiegogo, or Patreon allow filmmakers to tap into a broader base of "vanity" or fan-driven investors.

I'm currently working on a separate book that focuses on crowdfunding, so you may wish to look at that. I have put vanity players in the same category for today's purposes. But it's important to recognize that there are still quite a few differences between the two of them.

Vanity investors are typically people who will get involved in your project because they want the reward of either advancing their career in the film business (often as an actor, producer, or some other role in the creation of the film) or they want credit in the film to impress others or fulfill a personal aspiration.

How to locate and engage these groups:

- *Conventions and fan events:* Film conventions attract individuals eager to participate in projects or support films they are excited about.

- *Social Media:* Platforms like Instagram, Twitter, TikTok, and Facebook allow direct engagement with fans and supporters.

- *Online Communities:* Forums, fan groups, and niche websites can help you identify people who are highly enthusiastic about your type of film.

Crowdfunding or vanity players is not just about the money—it also creates an early audience, which is valuable for marketing and building momentum.

6. Trade Shows and Industry Events

Trade shows and industry events often attract individuals or companies looking for exposure and connections. These people may contribute cash, products, or services that can offset costs in your production.

- Attend trade shows relevant to your film's genre or audience.

- Identify exhibitors and attendees who might benefit from association with your project.

- Consider how your project provides visibility, networking, or marketing opportunities for them.

Trade shows are also excellent for building relationships that may lead to multiple types of support, including sponsorship, product placement, or collaborative ventures.

7. Pitching Events

Pitching events function similarly to "*Shark Tank*" style presentations for films. They provide an opportunity to showcase your project to multiple potential funders in a short period.

Tips for participating in pitching events:

- *Research the legitimacy of the event before participating. Check past participants, success stories, and organizers.*

- *Tailor your pitch to the audience and their motivations.*

- *Prepare concise, clear materials highlighting risk mitigation, budget, and potential returns.*

- *Practice answering questions that investors may ask about both creative and business aspects.*

Pitching events can accelerate the funding process by providing direct access to multiple potential partners in one venue.

HINT: Remember that pitching events are very much like a competition. You will be competing against several others when it comes to finding the funding you are looking for. I always recommend my students set the goal of their pitch to be setting up a second meeting that takes place in another setting and another time, far away from the pitching event. This helps you to bring your project into a stronger, less competitive environment where the potential film funding partner will not be distracted by whatever wonderful pitch will follow yours.

8. Filmmaker Contests and Festivals

Contests, labs, and festivals can provide both funding and third-party validation. Winning or participating in these competitions signals to potential funders that your project has been vetted and recognized by industry professionals.

- Seek out filmmaker labs that offer grants, mentoring, or other forms of support.

- Participate in competitions to build credibility and gain exposure.

- *Use awards and recognition as third-party endorsements, which make funding partners more comfortable investing in your project.*

This dual benefit, financial support and credibility, can significantly increase your chances of attracting larger, long-term investors.

HINT: *Most potential film funding partners don't know much about the different film festivals and filmmaker events that exist. Any win in even a small festival or contest may seem impressive to them and add credibility to your project.*

9. Qualifying Potential Funding Partners

Before meeting with anyone, it is essential to qualify potential film funding partners. Not all funders are suitable for every project. Qualification ensures your time and energy are spent on individuals or organizations that are capable, motivated, and aligned with your project.

Factors to consider:

- *Financial Capacity:* Can they contribute at the level you require?

- *Motivation:* Are they interested in financial return, creative participation, philanthropy, or marketing exposure?

- *Authority:* Do they have the ability to approve funding?

- *Alignment:* Does your project resonate with their goals, values, or brand?

- *Track Record:* Have they funded similar projects in the past?

By qualifying funders in advance, you avoid wasting time and focus on high-potential opportunities.

Questions Filmmakers Should Ask

1. *What type of potential funder is most aligned with my project (institutional, individual, philanthropic, fan-based, sponsor)?*

2. *How do I identify people who have both the capacity and desire to fund my project?*

3. *Where do potential funders spend time (events, conventions, online communities)?*

4. *How do I research the past funding behavior of potential partners?*

5. *What motivates each potential funder?*

6. *How can I connect my project to their personal or professional goals?*

7. *Who do I know personally that might be interested?*

8. *Who might they know that could also be interested?*

9. *Which trade shows or industry events are relevant for connecting with funders?*

10. Are there conventions or fan events where my audience is active?

11. What crowdfunding platforms are most suitable for my type of project?

12. How do I identify legitimate pitching events?

13. How should I prepare differently for pitching events versus one-on-one meetings?

14. Are there filmmaker contests or labs that offer funding or mentoring?

15. How do I use awards or recognition to strengthen credibility with funders?

16. How can I segment my potential funders based on motivation and type?

17. What type of pitch materials will resonate with each group?

18. *How do I balance the number of funders versus total contributions required?*

19. *How do I qualify funders before meeting them?*

20. *What red flags indicate a potential funder may not be suitable?*

21. *How can I leverage social media to identify fans and crowdfunding supporters?*

22. *How do I approach brands or sponsors for product placement or marketing partnerships?*

23. *What combination of funding sources will maximize my project's success?*

24. *How do I maintain relationships with funders even if they cannot contribute immediately?*

25. *How can I continually expand my network to include new funding opportunities?*

10. Practical Suggestions for Finding Funding Partners

1. **Create a detailed funding profile:** Understand their capacity, motivation, influence, and network.

2. **Map your network:** Include friends, family, industry contacts, and indirect connections.

3. **Use institutional sources first:** They are easier to locate and have clear criteria.

4. **Leverage conventions and trade shows:** Connect with vanity investors, sponsors, and fans.

5. **Engage with social media and online communities:** Identify crowdfunding supporters and enthusiastic fans.

6. **Participate in pitching events and competitions:** Gain access to multiple funders and third-party validation.

7. **_Qualify funders before meetings:_** _Focus on those with both resources and alignment with your project._

8. **_Personalize your pitch:_** _Different funders require different approaches based on motivation._

9. **_Use recognition strategically:_** _Awards, lab participation, and contests build credibility._

10. **_Track and expand your network continuously:_** _Every successful interaction can lead to new funding opportunities._

Finding funding partners is not about luck; it is about research, strategy, and relationship-building.

By understanding who has the money, where they can be found, and how to approach them effectively, you increase your chances of raising the funds needed to make your film a reality. The more prepared and intentional you are, the easier it becomes to connect with the right

people and secure the resources necessary to bring your

vision to life.

Chapter 8

HOW TO CONVINCE THEM

Raising money for a film is as much about persuasion, vision, and connection as it is about numbers and budgets. By this stage, you've already identified potential film funding partners, understood their motivations, and prepared your pitch. The next critical step is convincing them to participate, not by pressuring or coercing, but by aligning your project with what they value most.

This chapter explores how to communicate your project's value, mitigate risk, and inspire confidence, while finding the right people who are excited about your film as much as you are.

Convincing funders is part sales job, part inspiration, and entirely about relationship-building and alignment.

1. Understanding What Your Project Contributes

Before you can convince anyone to fund your film, you must be crystal clear on what your project contributes and to whom. Funders are not just giving money, they are investing in the potential of your idea, your ability to deliver it, and the value it creates for them.

Consider these aspects:

- *Artistic Value:* What unique creative or narrative contribution does your film make?

- *Financial Potential:* How can the film generate revenue, and what are the realistic returns?

- *Audience Impact:* Who will find this project compelling or meaningful?

- *Personal Alignment:* How does the project align with the funder's interests or goals?

When you can articulate the contribution of your project, you are no longer asking for money, you are offering an opportunity.

2. Part Sales Job, Part Inspiration

Convincing funders is a hybrid skill. It combines sales techniques with inspirational storytelling.

- *The sales component ensures funders understand the tangible aspects of your project: budget, timeline, risk mitigation, and potential returns.*

- *The inspirational component communicates why your project matters, what excites you as the filmmaker, and why it should excite them.*

Many filmmakers focus solely on the inspirational side, assuming passion alone will attract funding. Others rely only on numbers and structure, failing to convey the creative vision. The most effective approach balances both.

3. Mitigating Risk

Funders are inherently cautious, they want to know that their contribution is safe and well-managed. Part of convincing them involves mitigating perceived risks:

- **Financial Risk:** Show how funds will be allocated, how returns are projected, and any safeguards in place.

- **Creative Risk:** Demonstrate your ability to execute the project successfully, including experience, team structure, and past successes.

- **Time Risk:** Outline a realistic production schedule with milestones and contingencies.

- **Outcome Risk:** Discuss what happens if the project does not go as planned, and how you intend to respond.

By addressing risk upfront, you build credibility and trust. Funders are far more likely to invest when they feel confident that their investment is protected and managed professionally.

4. Shifting Beliefs: Strengthening Commitment

A key aspect of convincing funders is shifting beliefs. The stronger their belief in your project, the stronger their commitment will be.

- **Demonstrate Potential:** Show what the project can achieve artistically, financially, or culturally.

- **Share Your Vision:** Help them see the success you are envisioning.

- **Build Confidence:** Provide evidence through past projects, awards, or testimonials that demonstrate your ability to deliver.

When funders truly believe in the project and believe in you, they are far more likely to commit.

5. Helping Others See the Vision

One of the most important skills a filmmaker can develop is the ability to help others see the vision. Funders often need to see what excites you in order to feel inspired themselves.

Focus on what funders want to see:

- ***Potential to make money:*** Even vanity or philanthropic investors appreciate knowing there is a tangible upside.

- ***Artistic Vision:*** Convey why this project is unique and why it matters creatively.

- ***Successful Outcome:*** Help funders envision the finished film and the recognition, impact, or success it will achieve.

The goal is not to convince them at all costs, it is to identify funders who resonate with your vision naturally.

6. Highlighting Your Past Track Record

One of the most persuasive tools you have is your track record. Funders want to know they are backing a filmmaker who has demonstrated the ability to deliver.

- *Highlight completed projects, budgets managed, or previous successes.*

- *If possible, show measurable outcomes, such as awards, box office results, audience reach, or critical acclaim.*

- *Demonstrate growth: how each past project prepared you to make this current film even more successful.*

Your track record is proof of competence and can reduce perceived risk, making funders more comfortable committing.

7. Finding Funders Who Already Like Your Idea

It's important to recognize that convincing funders is not about persuading everyone. Not every person will resonate with your project, and that is perfectly fine. Your goal is to find those who already like your idea, even if for different reasons than you.

- Vanity investors may love the participation opportunities.

- Institutional investors may focus on financial upside.

- Fans may support the creative vision itself.

Rather than trying to convert everyone, focus your energy on funders whose interests align with your project, as they will be naturally inclined to say yes.

Questions Filmmakers Should Ask

Here are 25 critical questions filmmakers should ask themselves:

1. Who will find my project valuable and why?

2. *What aspects of my project are most compelling to funders?*

3. *Am I presenting both the creative and financial aspects effectively?*

4. *How can I inspire belief in the project without overselling?*

5. *How can I demonstrate that risks are minimized and managed?*

6. *What evidence from my past track record can support my pitch?*

7. *Which funders are already likely to be excited about my project?*

8. *How do I identify the motivations of each potential funder?*

9. *How much detail do I need to provide to satisfy risk concerns?*

10. *How can I present my vision in a way that funders can see themselves benefiting?*

11. *How do I communicate confidence without arrogance?*

12. *Which funders are motivated by financial return versus personal satisfaction?*

13. *How can I make the potential success of my project tangible?*

14. *How do I handle objections or doubts professionally?*

15. *What stories or examples can I share to illustrate potential outcomes?*

16. *How do I balance inspiring belief with realistic expectations?*

17. *How much of the pitch should focus on me versus the project?*

18. *Which aspects of the project might resonate most with specific funders?*

19. *How do I avoid overpromising while still inspiring excitement?*

20. *How can I engage funders in a dialogue about the project's potential?*

21. *What follow-up materials can reinforce belief and commitment?*

22. *How do I ensure that funders understand both the creative vision and business plan?*

23. *Which funders are more responsive to passion, and which to data?*

24. *How can I leverage endorsements or testimonials to strengthen credibility?*

25. *How do I determine if a funder is aligned enough to pursue a relationship further?*

8. Practical Suggestions and Strategies

1. ***Map the value proposition:*** *Be clear about what your project contributes and why funders should care.*

2. ***Balance inspiration and facts:*** *Combine a compelling narrative with concrete financial and operational details.*

3. ***Address Risk Upfront:*** *Show funders you have considered and mitigated potential pitfalls.*

4. ***Leverage Past Successes:*** *Highlight previous projects, measurable results, or relevant experience.*

5. ***Identify Aligned Funders:*** *Focus on those whose motivations naturally match your project.*

6. ***Customize your pitch:*** *Tailor your message to each funder's interests, goals, and level of engagement.*

7. ***Use visuals and storytelling:*** *Help funders see the final product and the impact it will have.*

8. *Communicate confidence and preparedness:* Funders invest in people as much as ideas.

9. *Encourage belief, not pressure:* Inspire funders to feel excited and motivated, rather than coerced.

10. *Follow up thoughtfully:* Reinforce confidence through updates, clarifications, and ongoing communication.

9. Key Takeaways

- *Convincing funders is a mix of salesmanship, vision, and credibility.*

- *Funders are motivated by different things: financial return, personal satisfaction, creative alignment, or impact.*

- *Your job is to help them see the potential, minimize risk, and build trust.*

- *It's not about convincing everyone—it's about finding funders who resonate naturally with your project.*

- *Past track record, preparation, and clear communication are essential tools in inspiring confidence and commitment.*

By mastering the art of convincing funders, you move from simply asking for money to offering an opportunity, one that aligns their goals with your vision, reduces their risk, and inspires them to be part of something meaningful and successful. This chapter emphasizes that convincing funders is not a manipulative exercise. It's a strategic combination of understanding motivations, communicating value, demonstrating competence, and inspiring belief. Funders are most likely to invest when they feel aligned with the project and confident in the filmmaker leading it. The stronger their belief in the vision and the person behind it, the stronger their commitment becomes.

Chapter 9

DOING THE DEAL

Raising funds for a film is only half the battle. The real challenge, and the place where projects succeed or fail, comes when it's time to formalize the agreement. "Doing the deal" is about turning potential funders into partners by structuring an exchange that creates value for all parties while minimizing risk. This stage transforms interest and commitment into tangible agreements that allow your film to move from idea to production.

In this chapter, we will explore the elements of a film deal, what funders are seeking, how to mitigate risk, and practical ways to structure agreements that satisfy all parties.

1. Funding as an Exchange

It is essential to understand that **funding is an exchange,** not a one-way transaction. Funders give resources—typically money—but in return, they expect **value.** Value is subjective and can take many forms:

- **Equity:** A share of profits or ownership in the project.

- **Interest on a loan:** A financial return for lending money.

- **Film credits:** Recognition on screen as an investor, producer, or contributor.

- **Participation opportunities:** Acting roles, involvement in production, or creative input.

- **Merchandise or brand association:** Co-branding opportunities or exposure in marketing materials.

- **Exclusive access:** Invitations to premieres, screenings, or behind-the-scenes experiences.

A successful deal occurs when the value given matches the expectations of the funder, and when the filmmaker is also clear on what is being exchanged.

2. Understanding the Goals of Potential Film Funding Partners

Every funder has goals—sometimes overlapping, sometimes unique. Understanding these goals is critical to structuring a deal that works for both parties.

Potential goals may include:

- ***Financial Returns:*** *Profit from box office, streaming, or other revenue streams.*

- ***Creative Involvement:*** *Participation in the project, influence on decisions, or personal satisfaction.*

- ***Recognition or Prestige:*** *Credits, association with successful projects, or industry visibility.*

- ***Brand Exposure:*** *Marketing opportunities for companies or products.*

- *Personal fulfillment:* Contributing to meaningful content, supporting a cause, or achieving a lifelong dream.

By identifying and aligning your approach with these goals, you can craft deals that funders perceive as high-value exchanges, making them more likely to commit.

3. What Is a Deal?

At its core, a deal is an agreement between two or more parties regarding contributions, expectations, and outcomes. In film funding, a deal typically includes:

1. ***Contribution:*** The specific resources provided by the funder—money, services, or other support.

2. ***Expectation:*** What the funder will receive in return, whether it's equity, credit, recognition, or a share of profits.

3. **Terms:** *Timeline, conditions for return, participation rights, or repayment schedules.*

4. **Risk management:** *Measures to protect both the funder and the filmmaker from unforeseen circumstances.*

A well-structured deal benefits all parties and creates a clear roadmap for collaboration.

4. Legal Considerations

Formalizing a deal requires legal guidance. Lawyers and legal advisors ensure that agreements are binding, clear, and enforceable. Key legal considerations include:

- *Drafting contracts that outline contributions, expectations, and responsibilities.*

- *Ensuring compliance with securities and investment regulations.*

- *Protecting intellectual property rights.*

- *Addressing dispute resolution and contingencies.*

- *Documenting repayment or profit-sharing terms.*

Legal assistance transforms verbal agreements into structured partnerships, reducing misunderstandings and protecting everyone involved.

5. Mitigating Risk

Risk mitigation is a crucial part of structuring any film deal. Funders are naturally cautious, and addressing potential risks builds confidence.

Common risk mitigation strategies include:

- *Transparent budgeting and financial planning.*

- *Clear timelines and milestones.*

- *Contingency planning for delays, overruns, or creative changes.*

- *Defined exit strategies if the project cannot proceed.*

- *Legal agreements protecting both parties' interests.*

By demonstrating awareness and preparation, filmmakers can turn perceived risk into trust, which often accelerates funding commitments.

6. Transitioning From Funder to Partner

When a deal is made, a potential film funding partner transitions into a real partner. This partnership goes beyond a financial transaction—it often involves:

- *Collaboration on marketing or distribution strategies.*

- *Advisory or creative input on the project.*

- *Long-term engagement that may influence future projects.*

Treating funders as partners strengthens relationships and builds a foundation for future collaborations and ongoing support.

7. Determining What to Offer

There are countless ways to create value for a funder. What you offer depends on your project, the funder's goals, and your negotiation approach.

Options include:

- **Equity:** Shares in profits or ownership in the film entity.

- **Loan Interest:** Returns based on financial agreements.

- **Film Credits:** Associate the funder's name with the project.

- **Participation opportunities:** Acting roles, set visits, or production involvement.

- **Merchandise or licensing:** Brand inclusion in promotional materials.

- **Recognition Events:** Invitations to premieres, panels, or private screenings.

The key is to offer something meaningful that aligns with their goals while protecting your interests and your creative vision.

HINT: One of the great questions I always ask a potential film funding partner that helps you see if they're ready to go and how close you are is to ask, "If you were to get involved as a funding partner in this project, what else would you need to make the deal work?" This always sets the conversation up to conclude with a very clear yes or no.

8. Structuring the Deal

A well-structured deal addresses three main questions:

1. **What is being exchanged?** Clearly define contributions and what the funder receives in return.

2. **How will it work?** Outline timelines, milestones, and reporting requirements.

3. ***What happens if things don't go as planned?*** Include contingencies, exit strategies, and risk mitigation measures.

Structuring a deal is not just about satisfying funders, it's about protecting your project, your creative vision, and your future relationships.

HINT: One key that has really helped close a lot of deals is to offer to put the funds into some kind of escrow or controlled account where the funds are only released to you as a filmmaker at certain stages of production or only if certain requirements are met. This helps a potential film funding partner feel that their money is somewhat safer, and progress on the project is part of the agreement.

Questions Filmmakers Should Ask

1. What does the funder value most—financial return, creative involvement, or recognition?

2. How much are they willing to contribute, and on what terms?

3. What type of return or recognition do they expect?

4. Are they interested in equity, a loan, or another form of participation?

5. What legal structures are required to formalize the agreement?

6. How will we document contributions and expectations?

7. What contingencies should we include in case of delays or unforeseen circumstances?

8. How much control or influence will the funder have in the project?

9. Are there intellectual property considerations to address?

10. *How will profits or returns be calculated and distributed?*

11. *What is the funder's risk tolerance?*

12. *What are the key milestones for funding release?*

13. *How will disagreements or disputes be resolved?*

14. *What communication and reporting will the funder require?*

15. *What is the process for amending the deal if circumstances change?*

16. *Are there tax implications for the funder or the project?*

17. *How do we ensure all parties understand their obligations?*

18. *How much negotiation flexibility exists on either side?*

19. *What additional incentives can be offered to align interests?*

20. *How can we protect creative control while satisfying funder expectations?*

21. *Are there industry standards or templates we can reference?*

22. *What steps ensure the deal is enforceable legally?*

23. *How can we structure deals for multiple funders simultaneously?*

24. *How do we manage funders who want to participate actively versus passively?*

25. *How will completing this deal position us for future funding opportunities?*

9. Practical Suggestions and Strategies for Doing the Deal

1. ***Understand funder goals:*** *Ensure what you offer aligns with what they value.*

2. **Be transparent:** Clearly outline contributions, expectations, and risks.

3. **Seek legal guidance early:** Avoid ambiguity and protect both parties.

4. **Mitigate risk proactively:** Demonstrate professionalism and preparedness.

5. **Structure value exchanges thoughtfully:** Use credits, equity, participation, or recognition strategically.

6. **Communicate milestones and timelines:** Give funders confidence in progress and outcomes.

7. **Treat funders as partners:** Foster relationships that extend beyond a single project.

8. **Tailor the deal individually:** Each funder has unique motivations and risk tolerance.

9. **Include contingencies:** Plan for delays, budget overruns, or changes in creative direction.

10. ***Document everything:*** *Ensure contracts are clear, enforceable, and understood by all parties.*

11. ***Use the deal as a foundation for future projects:*** *Strong, transparent deals build long-term trust and open doors for additional funding.*

10. Key Takeaways

- *Funding is an exchange, not a donation. Funders expect value, whether financial, creative, or reputational.*

- *Structuring a deal transforms a potential funder into a partner, strengthening collaboration and long-term support.*

- *Legal guidance is essential to protect all parties and ensure enforceability.*

- *Mitigating risk and understanding funder goals increases confidence and commitment.*

- *Deals can include equity, loans, participation, recognition, merchandising, or brand association. Choose what best aligns with your project and their expectations.*

- *Well-structured deals not only fund the current project but also build credibility for future projects.*

Successfully "doing the deal" requires preparation, transparency, and a focus on creating win-win situations. By understanding what funders value, addressing risk, and formalizing agreements professionally, filmmakers can secure the resources they need while establishing long-term relationships that extend beyond a single project.

Chapter 10

REPORTING AND ACCOUNTING

Once a film is funded, the work does not stop with production. In fact, some of the most important aspects of successfully managing funding come after the money has been received. Proper reporting and accounting are crucial for maintaining trust, managing relationships, and preparing the groundwork for future funding opportunities. Funders are not only providing resources, but they are investing in you, your project, and your ability to deliver.

By demonstrating professionalism in how you manage funds and communicate progress, you reinforce your credibility and reputation in the industry.

This chapter explores the importance of communication, consistency, expectation management, and accounting practices as tools to strengthen relationships with your film funding partners.

1. The Importance of Communication

Clear, timely, and transparent communication is the backbone of all successful funding relationships. Reporting is not just a bureaucratic exercise, it is a way to keep funders connected to the vision and inspired by the project's progress.

- *Regular updates show funders that their contribution is being actively managed.*

- *Transparency about challenges or delays builds trust rather than eroding it.*

- *Sharing milestones and successes reinforces the belief in the project's potential.*

Funders who feel informed and connected are more likely to continue supporting your current and future projects.

It's also important to mention that communication will include sharing bad news, too. Remember that once there is an agreement with a film funding partner, they are your partner. My experience has been that if there is bad news to report, the film funding partner is much more likely to help you if they know what's going on. It is important to remember that for the most part, your new partner will have experience in business and investment, and experiencing a hick up will not be something new. Often, sharing these challenges clearly and openly with your funding partners can create insights for solutions you may not have considered, not to mention the trust that it will create for future projects.

2. Consistency Matters

Consistency in reporting is as important as communication itself. Inconsistent updates, irregular reporting, or sporadic contact can erode trust and leave funders uncertain about the project's management.

- Establish a reporting schedule at the outset (weekly, monthly, quarterly).

- Decide on formats and channels—email summaries, detailed accounting reports, or virtual meetings.

- Ensure the style and structure of reports are consistent so funders know what to expect.

Consistency not only builds confidence but also demonstrates professionalism and organizational competence.

3. Managing Expectations

One of the most delicate aspects of reporting is managing funder expectations. Early communication sets the tone for what funders will anticipate regarding progress, financial performance, and creative outcomes.

- *Be realistic about timelines, deliverables, and potential obstacles.*

- *Avoid overpromising or presenting overly optimistic projections.*

- *Clarify what information funders can expect in reports and how often it will be provided.*

By managing expectations, you reduce surprises and prevent frustration, which is critical for maintaining long-term relationships.

4. Managing Relationships Through Reporting

Reporting is not only about numbers and progress, but it is also a relationship management tool. Funders are more likely to stay engaged if they feel respected, included, and valued.

- *Address funders personally in updates rather than using generic messaging.*

- *Highlight their contribution and the role it plays in the success of the project.*

- *Solicit feedback and answer questions promptly.*

- *Share achievements and milestones, giving funders a sense of ownership and pride.*

Properly managed reporting turns funders into partners, and these relationships can lead to future funding opportunities or referrals to other potential partners.

5. Reporting as a Tool to Keep the Vision Alive

Reporting is not simply about numbers; it is also a way to keep the project's vision alive for funders. Often, funders contribute because they believe in the story, mission, or impact of the film. Regular updates remind them why they became involved in the first place:

- *Include narrative updates about progress in production or post-production.*

- *Share creative milestones such as casting announcements, scene completion, or behind-the-scenes stories.*

- *Highlight audience engagement, social media traction, or festival entries.*

By connecting reporting to the larger purpose and vision of the project, you maintain enthusiasm and strengthen commitment.

6. Accounting Considerations

Accurate and transparent accounting is a critical component of reporting. Funders expect to know how their money is being managed and spent. Proper accounting practices ensure clarity, prevent misunderstandings, and protect both the filmmaker and funders legally.

- *Identify who will manage accounting: Ensure they understand both accounting principles and the nuances of film production finance.*

- *Track expenses diligently: Maintain detailed records of every expenditure and income source.*

- *Provide accessible reports: Funders should easily understand how funds were allocated and spent.*

- *Integrate production milestones with financial reporting: Show how spending aligns with progress.*

*Proper accounting builds confidence that funds are **being managed responsibly,** which strengthens trust and credibility.*

7. Choosing the Right Accounting Support

It is vital to assign accounting responsibilities to someone who understands the specific demands of film financing:

- Experienced film accountants or financial advisors familiar with industry norms are ideal. Having someone help you who has experience with film will be an incredible asset. Not only will they understand how to create reports, but they may also have insights into how you can take advantage of various government and tax incentives and support structures.

- If using a general accountant, ensure they are trained on budget categories, production schedules, and fund allocation.

- Funders are more likely to trust reporting from someone who demonstrates experience and competence in film accounting.

Choosing the right person to manage funds ensures accuracy, clarity, and funder confidence·

8. Delivering Reports Effectively

How you deliver reports can impact how funders perceive your project and professionalism:

- *Written reports: Include both narrative updates and detailed financial statements·*

- *Meetings or calls: Supplement written reports with discussions to address questions and highlight progress·*

- *Dashboards or visual reporting tools: Present budgets, milestones, and projections in an easy-to-read format·*

Reports should inform, reassure, and inspire, not overwhelm with unnecessary complexity·

Questions Filmmakers Should Ask

Who will manage accounting for the project, and what experience do they have?

1. *How often should I report to funders—weekly, monthly, quarterly?*

2. *What level of detail should each report include?*

3. *How can I ensure reports are consistent over time?*

4. *What communication channels are most effective for reporting?*

5. *How do I manage expectations if a milestone is delayed?*

6. *How should I structure narrative updates to keep the vision alive?*

7. *What financial metrics are most important to funders?*

8. *How do I track expenses and income accurately during production?*

9. *How should accounting software or tools be used for clarity?*

10. *What is the best way to report unexpected challenges or cost overruns?*

11. *How do I balance transparency with brevity in reports?*

12. *What format will funders find most understandable, spreadsheets, dashboards, or narrative summaries?*

13. *How can I highlight funders' contributions effectively?*

14. *How do I integrate production milestones with financial reporting?*

15. *Should I schedule calls or meetings to review reports?*

16. *How do I ensure funders feel included without micromanaging them?*

17. *How should I respond if a funder disagrees with a spending decision?*

18. *How do I prepare for audits or financial reviews?*

19. *Who is responsible for ensuring reports are accurate and complete?*

20. *How do I communicate the impact or results of expenditures to funders?*

21. *How can I create visual reporting tools that are easy to interpret?*

22. *How do I handle confidential or sensitive financial information?*

23. *How can reporting strengthen relationships for future projects?*

24. *How do I ensure consistency if multiple people are responsible for reporting or accounting?*

9. Practical Suggestions and Strategies

1. **Establish a reporting schedule at the outset:** *Set expectations early for frequency, format, and content.*

2. **Combine narrative and financial reporting:** Use updates to share creative milestones alongside financial transparency.

3. **Select experienced accounting support:** Choose someone knowledgeable in film finances to maintain credibility.

4. **Use Visual Tools:** Charts, dashboards, and graphs can make financial data easier to understand.

5. **Highlight funder contributions:** Recognize their role in updates, events, or screenings.

6. **Be transparent about challenges:** Share obstacles honestly while presenting solutions and next steps.

7. **Link spending to outcomes:** Show how funds are advancing the project toward completion.

8. **Provide summaries and details:** Include both high-level and detailed reporting to meet varying funder needs.

12. *Incorporate audience and project metrics:* Reporting isn't only financial; show engagement and impact.

13. *Foster ongoing communication:* Encourage questions and feedback to strengthen relationships.

14. *Keep historical records:* Maintain an archive of reports for accountability and lessons learned.

15. *Prepare for audits or funder reviews:* Being organized protects credibility and supports future funding.

16. *Use reporting as a marketing tool:* Highlight milestones publicly when appropriate to maintain visibility.

17. *Adjust based on funder preferences:* Some may prefer written reports; others prefer video or in-person updates.

18. ***Plan for continuity:*** *If someone leaves your team, ensure reporting responsibilities are well documented.*

10. Key Takeaways

- *Reporting and accounting are not just administrative tasks—they are relationship management tools.*

- *Consistency, transparency, and clarity in reporting build trust with funders.*

- *Reporting connects funders to the vision and impact of your project, reinforcing why they invested.*

- *Choosing the right accounting support ensures credibility and accuracy.*

- *Well-structured, clear, and frequent reporting improves satisfaction, strengthens relationships, and increases the likelihood of future funding.*

- Treat reporting as an opportunity to celebrate milestones, demonstrate progress, and show the value of funders' contributions.

Ultimately, effective reporting and accounting protect your project, maintain trust, and position you for ongoing success in funding future films. Funders want to feel informed, appreciated, and confident that their investment is being used wisely. Your reporting ensures this happens.

Chapter 11

WORKING WITH INVESTORS BEYOND THE FILM

Securing funding for a single film is a significant accomplishment, but the real power in filmmaking lies in building lasting relationships with your investors. The most successful filmmakers don't just chase new investors for each project; they cultivate long-term partnerships, maintain trust, and create repeat funding opportunities. By focusing on investors beyond the film, you can reduce the stress of constantly seeking new funding and establish a reliable network for multiple projects over time.

This chapter explores how to maintain investor relationships, keep them engaged, and leverage their satisfaction into future funding and referrals.

1. Keep Your Investors Instead of Always Finding New Ones

Many filmmakers make the mistake of thinking that funding is a one-time activity and that each new project requires entirely new investors. While diversification has value, it is often easier and more efficient to retain investors you've already worked with.

- *Returning investors already know your track record and work ethic.*

- *They trust your ability to deliver, reducing perceived risk.*

- *They may be willing to contribute more to subsequent projects, sometimes without needing as much convincing.*

By nurturing these relationships, you can create a reliable funding base that grows with your career.

2. Communication Is Key

Communication is the cornerstone of any strong relationship. Investors are not just putting money into a film—they are entrusting you with a piece of their resources and confidence.

Keeping them informed throughout and beyond the production is essential:

- **Regular Updates:** Keep them informed about the film's progress, distribution, and reception.

- **Personalized Engagement:** Reach out individually rather than sending generic emails.

- **Transparency:** Share both successes and challenges to maintain trust.

Consistent, meaningful communication reassures investors and keeps them invested in the journey, not just the project.

3. Consistency Builds Trust

Consistency in your interactions, reporting, and follow-ups is as critical as communication itself:

- *Regularly scheduled updates create predictability and reliability.*

- *Consistent messaging demonstrates professionalism and organizational skills.*

- *Investors who receive steady, clear, and honest information are more likely to invest in future projects.*

Consistency signals that you value their contribution and are dependable, which is vital in building long-term partnerships.

4. Participating in the Journey

Investors often want to participate in the journey, not just the outcome. Involving them in meaningful ways strengthens engagement and loyalty:

- *Invite them to key milestones such as premieres, special screenings, or production events.*

- *Share behind-the-scenes stories and progress updates.*

- *Allow for opportunities to provide input if appropriate, such as marketing ideas or networking introductions.*

Participation fosters a sense of ownership and connection, making investors more likely to return for future projects.

5. Ensuring Investor Goals Are Met

Investors are more likely to return if they feel their goals were achieved:

- ***Financial:*** *Did their contribution yield the expected financial returns?*

- ***Creative or reputational:*** *Were they recognized appropriately for their participation?*

- **_Personal satisfaction:_** _Did they enjoy the experience of being part of the project?_

Investors who see tangible or meaningful results from their involvement are naturally inclined to contribute again. Meeting or exceeding these expectations is crucial for building a loyal funding network.

6. Collect Feedback and Survey Investors

After a project concludes, it is important to ask investors for feedback:

- _Identify the most satisfying aspects of their experience._

- _Understand the challenges they faced during the funding or production process._

- _Discover how the experience could be improved for future collaborations._

Surveys and conversations provide insight into how to enhance your investor experience, increasing the likelihood they will participate again or refer others to your projects.

7. Asking for Referrals

Many investors are hesitant to recommend new projects or filmmakers until they have experienced success themselves. Referrals can be a powerful source of funding, but only after trust is established:

- Start with smaller contributions if necessary; let new investors see that your system works.

- Demonstrate transparency, efficiency, and results with initial projects.

- Once they are satisfied, encourage referrals to friends, family, or colleagues.

Referrals often bring in investors who already have confidence in you, reducing the time and effort required to convince them.

8. Building Long-Term Relationships

Working beyond a single project requires relationship management:

- *Keep in touch with investors even when you are not actively seeking funding.*

- *Share relevant news about your career, industry insights, or future projects.*

- *Recognize and celebrate milestones, awards, or releases to maintain engagement.*

The more investors feel connected to your work and your journey, the more likely they are to become repeat supporters and ambassadors for your films.

Questions Filmmakers Should Ask

1. *How can I keep investors engaged after a project is completed?*

2. *What frequency of communication is ideal for long-term relationships?*

3. *How do I maintain transparency without overwhelming investors?*

4. *How do I know if investor goals were truly achieved?*

5. *How can I measure investor satisfaction?*

6. *What feedback mechanisms can I use to improve future projects?*

7. *How do I personalize communication for each investor?*

8. *What milestones should investors be invited to beyond the film's release?*

9. *How can I involve investors in meaningful ways without compromising creative control?*

10. *What incentives or recognition strategies work best for long-term engagement?*

11. *How do I identify which investors are likely to invest again?*

12. *How can I turn satisfied investors into advocates for future projects?*

13. *What is the best way to request referrals from existing investors?*

14. *How do I ensure investors feel their contribution is valued?*

15. *How do I handle investors who have had a challenging experience?*

16. *What ongoing updates are meaningful without being burdensome?*

17. *How do I balance communication with multiple investors?*

18. *How can I demonstrate growth and improvement to returning investors?*

19. *What types of events or experiences increase investor loyalty?*

20. *How do I manage expectations for repeat investments?*

21. *How do I record and track feedback for future use?*

22. *How do I maintain professionalism while building personal rapport?*

23. *How can I showcase project success to attract repeat investments?*

24. *How do I identify potential investors who may start with small contributions?*

25. *What strategies ensure that long-term investors feel part of the project's story?*

10. Practical Suggestions and Strategies

1. **Develop an investor retention plan:** *Think of investors as long-term partners rather than one-time contributors.*

2. **Schedule Ongoing Communication:** *Monthly updates, milestone announcements, or behind-the-scenes stories maintain engagement.*

3. **Create Personalized Recognition:** *Public credits, invitations to events, or exclusive access reinforce value.*

4. **Survey investors after each project:** *Use feedback to improve processes and satisfaction.*

5. **Address Challenges Proactively:** *Resolve any issues promptly to maintain trust.*

6. **Encourage Referrals Selectively:** *Ask investors to recommend others only after a successful experience.*

7. **Start small with new investors:** Let them see your system works before scaling contributions.

8. **Document Investor Preferences:** Keep track of their communication style, goals, and areas of interest.

9. **Celebrate Achievements:** Awards, screenings, or media coverage reinforce their sense of partnership.

10. **Provide insight into future projects:** Share your vision for upcoming films to pique interest in continued participation.

11. **Maintain Professional Relationships:** Balance personal rapport with accountability and clarity.

12. **Leverage Repeat Investors for Credibility:** When returning investors participate, new investors are more likely to follow.

13. ***Offer Participatory Opportunities:*** *Set visits, production insights, or networking events enhance connection.*

14. ***Be Transparent about Outcomes:*** *Show both successes and learnings, reinforcing reliability.*

15. ***Recognize Loyalty:*** *Consider offering tiered recognition or rewards for investors who participate multiple times.*

11. Key Takeaways

- *Long-term investor relationships reduce the need to constantly find new funding.*

- *Consistent communication, transparency, and engagement are essential for keeping investors happy.*

- *Participation and meaningful involvement create a sense of ownership and loyalty.*

- *Achieving investor goals and collecting feedback increases the likelihood of repeat investment.*

- *Referrals from satisfied investors are powerful, but only after they have experienced success with you.*

- *Treat investors as partners, not just funders; their continued satisfaction is an asset for future projects and sustainable funding.*

Investors are far more than sources of money, they are partners in your creative journey.

By nurturing these relationships, you create a funding network that grows with your career, enabling multiple projects with less effort and greater confidence.

Chapter 12

ADDITIONAL FUNDING RESOURCES

Funding a film is often thought of in the simplest terms: you need investors or a lender willing to provide money. While these sources are critical, there is a vast landscape of additional funding resources that can reduce financial risk, enhance your project, and demonstrate to potential film funding partners that you are prepared, resourceful, and creative.

In this chapter, we explore grants, tax incentives, non-monetary contributions, licensing deals, crowdfunding, special interest groups, presales, co-productions, film contests, and mentoring or incubator programs. Understanding and leveraging these resources can help *make your film financially feasible, more appealing to investors, and ultimately more successful.*

1. Grants for Film Projects

Grants are a common yet underutilized resource for filmmakers. They are often provided by arts councils, cultural organizations, or private foundations to support artistic expression, education, or social impact projects.

- *Why grants exist: Grants exist to promote art, culture, education, or social initiatives. Many organizations are willing to fund films that align with their mission or values.*

- *Philanthropic grants: These come from individuals or foundations with a specific cause close to their hearts. Personal development, social impact, environmental awareness, or cultural preservation are common grant themes.*

*Grants are valuable because they **do not require repayment** and can also add legitimacy to your project when presenting it to potential film funding partners.*

2. Tax Benefits and Incentives

*Choosing the right location for your production can significantly impact your budget. Many regions offer **tax credits, rebates, or incentives** for film production.*

- ***Financial Benefit:** Tax incentives reduce the overall cost of production, effectively stretching your budget further.*

- ***Investor Appeal:** Showing that you have researched and secured these incentives demonstrates your diligence and consideration of protecting investor funds.*

- ***Location Flexibility:** Filming in areas with tax benefits can also influence decisions regarding where scenes are shot, crew hired, and production logistics.*

Being knowledgeable about tax benefits signals **professionalism and strategic planning,** *which can make your project more appealing to funding partners·*

3. Support Without Money

Not all contributions need to be cash· Non-monetary support can significantly reduce costs:

- ***Equipment discounts or donations:*** *Companies often support independent filmmakers with discounted or free equipment· For instance, William F· White offered discounted gear, saving thousands of dollars while providing access to professional-level equipment·*

- ***Services and Resources:*** *Editing, sound, production design, catering, or other services can sometimes be donated or offered at reduced rates by those interested in supporting the arts·*

- ***Experience and advice:*** Knowledge from experienced professionals can save money and avoid costly mistakes. Mentorship or guidance is an undervalued form of funding that improves efficiency and project quality.

By thinking creatively about what people can contribute, you can reduce costs, enhance production quality, and make your project more appealing to investors.

4. Licensing and Revenue Opportunities

Licensing deals are another way to **mitigate investor risk** and demonstrate potential revenue:

- ***Product Licensing:*** Collaborating with brands or products for exposure or sponsorship can generate additional funding or value in-kind.

- **Demonstrated Revenue Potential:** *Licensing agreements can provide reassurance to investors that the project has avenues for return, reducing perceived risk.*

- **Integration into your Project:** *Whether in documentaries, features, or short films, licensing deals can be strategically integrated to enhance authenticity and appeal.*

Investors respond well to projects that show multiple streams of revenue or risk mitigation strategies, and licensing is a strong example of both.

5. Crowdfunding

Crowdfunding remains a powerful tool for filmmakers:

- **Audience Engagement:** *Crowdfunding campaigns not only raise money but also generate an early fan base for your film.*

- **_Social Proof:_** A successful crowdfunding campaign demonstrates that people are willing to support your project financially, reinforcing credibility for other funding partners.

- **_Creative Marketing:_** Platforms like Kickstarter, Indiegogo, or specialized niche crowdfunding websites allow for tiered contributions, rewards, and engagement opportunities.

Crowdfunding can be combined with other funding methods to **strengthen investor confidence** and reduce financial risk.

6. Special Interest Groups

Targeting specific groups that align with your film's themes can generate significant support:

- ***Audience Alignment:*** *Groups such as educational institutions, non-profits, or social organizations often fund projects aligned with their mission.*

- ***Personal development films example:*** *Catching groups, mothers'associations, businesses, and event organizers contributed to projects that resonated with their interests.*

- ***Community engagement:*** *Partnering with special interest groups builds relationships and can also assist with marketing and distribution.*

When approaching these groups, focus on how your project aligns with their goals, and offer opportunities for recognition or participation.

7. Presales and Co-Productions

Presales and co-productions are another method to reduce financial risk:

- **Presales:** Selling distribution rights in advance can provide cash flow during production. It requires a clear understanding of your target market, projected audience, and distribution strategy.

- **Co-productions:** Partnering with other filmmakers or production companies spreads both risk and cost. Co-producers can contribute resources, expertise, or access to markets that would otherwise be unavailable.

Both methods demonstrate to investors that the project has financial viability and market planning, increasing confidence in the potential success of the film.

8. Film Contests and Competitions

Participating in contests or filmmaker challenges can provide both **funding and recognition:**

- **Financial awards:** Many contests offer cash prizes for winners, which can supplement your budget.

- ***Third-party endorsement:*** *Winning awards or competitions adds credibility to your project, showing potential investors that your work is recognized for quality and innovation.*

- ***Exposure opportunities:*** *Contests often provide visibility in the industry and with audiences, which can lead to additional funding, partnerships, or distribution opportunities.*

*Contests and awards can be a strategic way to reduce risk **for investors** while enhancing your project's reputation.*

9. Mentoring, Labs, and Incubator Programs

Industry mentorship programs, labs, or incubators can be invaluable resources:

- *Guidance and training:* Programs provide advice on budgeting, pitching, production planning, and distribution.

- *Networking opportunities:* Access to industry professionals, potential funders, and collaborators can open doors that would otherwise be difficult to reach.

- *Resource access:* Some programs offer funding, equipment, or production resources as part of participation.

Participation in these environments demonstrates **commitment to professionalism** and can signal to potential funding partners that you are serious about producing a successful project.

10. Additional Potential Funding Resources

Beyond traditional investors, lenders, and the examples above, filmmakers can explore other creative funding sources:

- **Corporate sponsorships:** Companies may fund your project in exchange for brand exposure or alignment with their mission.

- **In-kind contributions:** Donations of goods or services from local businesses, restaurants, or community organizations.

- **Alumni Networks:** Universities or professional associations sometimes support alumni projects.

- **Arts organizations:** Cultural councils, film offices, and arts boards often have small project grants.

- **Trade associations:** Industry-specific organizations may support films aligned with their focus.

- **Local government or municipal grants:** Some cities have funds to encourage cultural production or tourism-related projects.

- **Non-Profit Partnerships:** Organizations interested in your project's theme may provide both financial and logistical support.

- **Online communities:** Niche groups on social media or forums sometimes pool resources to support independent projects.

- **International co-productions:** Foreign production companies can partner on projects with cross-market appeal.

- **Alumni crowdfunding platforms:** Universities, schools, or other organizations may facilitate campaigns for creative alumni.

- **Event partnerships:** Conferences, workshops, or community events may sponsor or promote your project in exchange for exposure.

- **Volunteer support:** Skilled volunteers can offset labor costs in areas like wardrobe, art, or production management.

- **Crowdsourcing expertise:** Platforms where professionals donate time or knowledge to help complete parts of the project.

- **Licensing or merchandising partnerships:** Selling branded merchandise tied to your project.

- **Product placement deals:** Companies may pay to feature their products in your film.

Questions Filmmakers Should

1. What grants are available for my genre or project type?

2. Are there philanthropic foundations aligned with my film's themes?

3. How do I qualify for tax incentives or credits in various locations?

4. What non-monetary contributions could significantly reduce my budget?

5. Which suppliers or organizations offer discounts or in-kind support for filmmakers?

6. How can experience or mentorship save costs or improve efficiency?

7. Are there licensing opportunities that could generate additional income?

8. How do I structure a crowdfunding campaign to maximize engagement?

9. Which special interest groups would find my project valuable?

10. What presale opportunities exist for my target market?

11. Which production companies are suitable co-production partners?

12. Are there film contests that could provide funding or recognition?

13. What labs, incubators, or mentorship programs could support my project?

14. How do I identify corporate sponsorship opportunities?

15. Can local arts boards or municipal programs provide financial or logistical support?

16. What online communities or niche networks could assist with funding?

17. How can international co-productions be structured to minimize risk?

18. Which volunteer or in-kind resources are feasible for my project?

19. How do I approach merchandising or product placement deals ethically?

20. What financial or creative benefits do presales offer?

21. How can I combine multiple alternative funding sources effectively?

22. Which of these resources provides the most credibility to potential investors?

23. How do I document non-monetary contributions for transparency?

24. Which funding opportunities align with the timeline and scale of my project?

25. How can I leverage these additional resources to attract traditional investors?

11. Suggestions and Strategies for Using Additional Funding Resources

1. ***Research thoroughly:*** *Identify all potential grants, tax benefits, and programs before planning your budget.*

2. ***Combine resources strategically:*** *Use grants, tax incentives, and in-kind contributions alongside investors to reduce risk.*

3. ***Demonstrate resourcefulness:*** *Showing potential funders that you have explored multiple avenues builds credibility.*

4. ***Engage community and special interest groups:*** *Their support can add both funding and marketing reach.*

5. ***Document all contributions:*** *Track both monetary and non-monetary support for transparency and reporting.*

6. ***Integrate crowdfunding as proof of demand:*** *Early audience support can validate your project for investors.*

7. ***Leverage contests and labs for credibility:*** *Awards and mentorship add third-party validation.*

8. ***Negotiate licensing or product placement deals:*** *These can both generate funds and reduce perceived risk.*

9. ***Use volunteer and in-kind contributions wisely:*** *Ensure quality and reliability while maximizing cost savings.*

10. ***Combine presales, co-productions, and grants:*** *Layering funding sources creates a more stable financial structure.*

11. ***Show investors your research:*** *Demonstrate tax incentives, grants, or sponsorship deals to reassure funders.*

12. *Maintain relationships with grant organizations:* Successful applications can lead to repeat funding for future projects.

13. **Create a matrix of resources:** Map potential funding sources, timelines, and contribution types to optimize planning.

14. **Consider smaller contributions strategically:** Multiple small resources can combine to cover substantial budget needs.

15. **Leverage success from alternative funding:** Show prior use of grants, tax credits, or sponsorships to attract larger investors.

12. Key Takeaways

- *Funding extends beyond investors or lenders; alternative resources can reduce costs, mitigate risk, and enhance investor confidence.*

- *Grants, tax incentives, and philanthropic support provide credibility and legitimacy.*

- *Non-monetary contributions, experience, licensing, and partnerships can save significant money and improve production quality.*

- *Crowdfunding, presales, co-productions, contests, and incubator programs can complement traditional funding and expand your network.*

- *A strategic combination of multiple funding sources demonstrates professionalism, resourcefulness, and reduces perceived risk for potential investors.*

- *Understanding and leveraging additional funding resources strengthens your ability to secure investor confidence, execute your project efficiently, and create a foundation for future filmmaking success.*

Chapter 13

PUTTING IT ALL TOGETHER: BUILDING A REPEATABLE FUNDING SYSTEM FOR FILMMAKERS

Filmmaking is a creative pursuit, but it is also a business. While many filmmakers focus solely on the artistry, the reality is that funding is the lifeblood of every project. Throughout this book, we've covered how to identify, approach, and work with potential film funding partners, as well as alternative funding resources and strategies. In this final chapter, we will pull all of these threads together, creating a repeatable system that enables filmmakers to consistently fund projects and build sustainable careers.

The goal of this chapter is simple: to help you think systematically about funding rather than relying on luck or ad hoc strategies. By the end of this chapter, you should understand how to structure your funding approach, maintain investor relationships, leverage alternative resources, and set yourself up for long-term success.

1. Start With a Clear Project Vision

Every successful funding system begins with clarity of vision. Potential film funding partners don't invest in ambiguity; they invest in a clear story—both on screen and behind the scenes.

Ask yourself:

- What is the core idea of my film?

- What makes it unique?

- Who will care about it, and why?

A clear vision provides a foundation for every subsequent step in your funding system. It is also the starting point for creating **pitch materials, identifying investors, and exploring alternative funding.**

2. Define Your Funding Needs Precisely

Once your project vision is clear, define the **exact funding needs:**

- How much money is required for production, marketing, and distribution?

- What is your timeline for needing funds?

- Which portions of the budget can be covered by grants, tax incentives, or alternative resources?

By creating a detailed budget that accounts for all aspects of the project, you not only show potential investors that you are prepared but also reduce the likelihood of unexpected shortfalls.

Remember: funding isn't a one-time activity. A well-defined budget also becomes the basis for future projects, enabling you to **repeat the process efficiently**.

3. Identify Potential Film Funding Partners Strategically

With a clear vision and budget, it's time to identify who can fund your project:

- Consider the range of potential film funding partners: investors, lenders, institutional money, philanthropists, crowdfunding participants, special interest groups, and corporate sponsors.

- Profile each potential partner to understand their goals, interests, and motivations.

- Don't assume someone will or will not invest; your task is to discover alignment between your project and their interests.

Maintaining a database or a profile system for potential partners allows you to track engagement, follow-ups, and feedback, making the process repeatable for future projects.

Build Your Pitch Materials With Investors in Mind

Pitching is not about showing off your creativity; it's about showing investors that you've thought through the business of filmmaking.

Effective pitch materials include:

- *Past successes and track record*

- *Detailed budget and timeline*

- *Risk mitigation strategies*

- *Project uniqueness and market potential*

- *Alternative funding and revenue opportunities*

*Think of your pitch materials as a **living system**. They can be adapted and reused for future projects, allowing* you to save time while continuously improving based on investor feedback.

Engage and Convince Investors Effectively

Once you've identified potential partners and prepared your pitch materials, the next step is **engagement:**

- *Focus on people who are excited about your project as much as you are.*

- *Present the project in a way that aligns with their motivations, whether artistic, financial, or personal.*

- *Mitigate risk through clear planning, alternative funding, and contingency strategies.*

Remember: funding is **part sales job, part inspiration.** Success comes from matching your project with the right people, not convincing everyone.

Secure the Deal and Formalize Agreements

With interest secured, you must move to **formalize the agreement:**

- Define what each party will contribute and receive.

- Ensure legal structures, contracts, and agreements are in place.

- Offer value beyond money: equity, credits, recognition, licensing opportunities, or participation.

A repeatable system includes standard legal and operational templates. These templates save time, reduce errors, and provide confidence to new investors that you are professional and trustworthy.

Maintain Communication and Reporting

Once funding is secured, communication is critical:

- Establish regular updates for investors.

- Track financials and project milestones.

- Manage expectations proactively.

Reporting is not just about accountability; it's about keeping investors connected to the vision. Regular updates make it easier to retain investors for future projects and to leverage referrals.

Nurture Long-Term Investor Relationships

The most valuable funding system is one where investors return for multiple projects:

- Keep investors engaged even when you're not actively raising funds.

- Celebrate successes and acknowledge contributions.

- Ask for feedback to improve the investor experience.

- Encourage referrals once trust and satisfaction are established.

A repeatable system emphasizes relationship-building over transactional interactions, creating a sustainable network of funding partners.

Leverage Alternative Funding Resources

Your funding system should include **diverse resources:**

- Grants and philanthropic funding

- Tax incentives and rebates

- In-kind support and equipment discounts

- Licensing, merchandising, or product placement deals

- Crowdfunding and special interest groups

- Presales and co-productions

- Film contests, incubators, and mentorship programs

Each of these resources reduces reliance on a single investor type, **mitigates risk,** and strengthens your appeal to potential partners.

Track and Analyze Your Funding Efforts

A repeatable system requires **metrics and analysis:**

- Which strategies yielded the most funding?

- *Which investors or groups responded best to your approach?*

- *Where did your process break down, and how can it be improved?*

*Documenting these insights allows you to **refine your system** and replicate success on subsequent projects, turning funding from a one-off struggle into a **repeatable, efficient process.***

Integrate Marketing and Distribution Into Your Funding System

Funding and marketing are interconnected:

- *Early engagement with audiences, crowdfunding supporters, or special interest groups creates both funds and fans.*

- *Pre-sales or distribution agreements can enhance investor confidence.*

* *Marketing materials and campaigns can also serve as pitch tools for new investors.*

*By considering marketing and distribution during the funding phase, you build a **holistic system** where every component supports both the creative and financial success of your film.*

Establish a Feedback Loop

*A repeatable funding system relies on **continuous improvement:***

* *After each project, evaluate what worked and what didn't.*

* *Update pitch materials, budgeting approaches, and communication strategies.*

* *Incorporate lessons from alternative funding sources, investor interactions, and marketing outcomes.*

Over time, this feedback loop creates a self-reinforcing system: each success builds credibility, streamlines processes, and increases the probability of securing funding for future projects.

Questions Filmmakers Should Ask

1. How can I create a funding system that works for multiple projects?

2. Which investors are most likely to return for future films?

3. How do I track communications, contributions, and agreements efficiently?

4. What combination of investors and alternative funding resources is optimal?

5. How do I standardize pitch materials for reuse?

6. What legal and contractual templates should I maintain?

7. *How can I maintain relationships with investors without constant fundraising?*

8. *How do I balance creative vision with financial strategy?*

9. *Which reporting methods keep investors satisfied and informed?*

10. *How do I integrate crowdfunding into a larger funding system?*

11. *What metrics should I track to evaluate funding effectiveness?*

12. *How do I leverage past successes to attract new investors?*

13. *How can I combine grants, tax incentives, and other resources with investor funding?*

14. *How do I identify potential film funding partners before pitching?*

15. *How do I manage multiple funding sources without confusion?*

16. *How can I ensure investors feel valued beyond financial return?*

17. *What systems can I use to track referrals from existing investors?*

18. *How do I integrate marketing and distribution planning into funding strategy?*

19. *How do I mitigate risk for each funding partner?*

20. *How do I decide which alternative funding sources to pursue for each project?*

21. *What follow-up process ensures investor engagement after the film is released?*

22. *How do I gather actionable feedback to improve future funding efforts?*

23. *How do I structure co-productions and presales for maximum benefit?*

24. *How do I maintain professional consistency across multiple projects?*

25. *What tools or platforms can support a repeatable, systematic funding approach?*

Practical Suggestions for Implementing a Repeatable System

1. *Maintain a central database of potential investors, alternative funding sources, and contacts.*

2. *Use standardized pitch templates, budgets, and contracts for efficiency.*

3. *Keep detailed records of communications, follow-ups, and contributions.*

4. *Develop a timeline for investor engagement that spans pre-production, production, and post-release.*

5. *Build feedback mechanisms to learn from each project and investor interaction.*

6. *Combine multiple funding sources for a diversified, resilient approach.*

7. *Incorporate marketing and audience engagement early to strengthen investor confidence.*

8. *Track results and metrics to optimize strategies for future projects.*

9. *Maintain a consistent relationship-building approach, focusing on long-term engagement.*

10. *Leverage successful past projects to validate your track record for new investors.*

Key Takeaways

- *Building a repeatable funding system transforms filmmaking from one-off funding struggles into a strategic, repeatable business.*

- *Start with a clear vision, precise budget, and strategic identification of potential funding partners.*

- *Pitch materials, communication, and investor engagement are core elements of the system.*

- *Alternative funding sources reduce risk, increase credibility, and complement traditional investors.*

- *Tracking, analysis, and feedback create continuous improvement, enhancing success over time.*

- *Long-term relationships, referrals, and repeat investors are the ultimate goal, providing a reliable network for multiple projects.*

By implementing this system, you are not simply chasing funding; you are creating a structured, repeatable process that enables sustained creative output, financial stability, and growth as a filmmaker. Each project builds credibility, strengthens your network, and brings you closer to a self-sustaining career in film.

Okay, so now you have new ideas, and you are ready.

Go get the funding and start making your movie.

About The Author

Douglas Vermeeren is an accomplished filmmaker, producer, and educator with extensive experience in raising funds for film projects of all sizes. He launched his career with the documentary feature *The Opus* in 2008, for which he successfully raised over $600,000. Following this, he has raised substantial funding for multiple documentaries, including *The Gratitude Experiment* (2013), *The Treasure Map* (2015), *How Thoughts Become Things* (2020), and *The Science of Getting Rich* (2024), establishing a track record of producing impactful personal development films that resonate with audiences worldwide.

In addition to his documentary work, Vermeeren has secured funding for numerous shorts and feature films, such as the award-winning short *Book of Dragons* (2025), and features including *Jackknife* (2023), *A Farewell to Youth* (2024), *Cowboy Bloodbath* (2025), and *The Baphomet Seance* (2025). His experience also spans television, having raised funds for shows like *The Video Games That Changed the World* and *Unexplained Paranormal Files*. Across all formats, Vermeeren has demonstrated an ability to connect with funding partners and bring diverse creative projects to life.

Beyond filmmaking, Vermeeren is a sought-after teacher and mentor in the field of film funding. He sits on the advisory board of the American Film Convention in Los Angeles and regularly leads seminars and training programs around the world, sharing strategies for securing financing and building sustainable careers in film. In addition to his work as an educator, he continues to actively pursue roles as an actor, producer, and director, combining practical experience with his teaching to guide the next generation of filmmakers.

For more information, go to www.DouglasVermeeren.com

You can also find him on IMDb.